THE HYMNS OF ORPHEUS

Orpheus plays the *vihuela*
from Luis Milan's *El Maestro*, 1536.

THE HYMNS
OF
ORPHEUS

Mutations by R. C. Hogart

PHANES PRESS
1993

98 97 96 95 94 93   5 4 3 2 1

Published by Phanes Press, PO Box 6114, Grand Rapids, Michigan 49516, USA.

PHANES PRESS publishes many fine books which relate to the philosophical, spiritual, and cosmological traditions of the Western world. To obtain a complete listing of our titles, please write to us at the above addess.

Library of Congress Cataloging-in-Publication Data

Orpheus.
      [Hymni. English]
      The hymns of Orpheus / mutations by R. C. Hogart.
         p.   cm.
      Includes bibliographical references.
      ISBN 0-933999-40-2 (alk. paper) — ISBN 0-933999-41-0
(pbk. : alk. paper)
      1. Hymns, Greek (Classical)—Translations into English. 2. Greek
poetry—Translations into English. 3. Gods, Greek—Poetry.
I. Hogart, Ron Charles, date.   II. Title
PA4259.E5   1993
881'.01—dc20   92-46247
                                                          CIP

This book is printed on alkaline paper which conforms to the permanent paper standard developed by the National Information Standards Organization.

Printed and bound in the United States of America

*

For Tamra.

Fate, Time, Occasion, Chance, and Change? To these
all things are subject but eternal Love.
—Shelley

Thanks to
Manly P. Hall, David Fideler, Kenneth Atchity,
Arthur Johnson, Renee Rumics,
Joseph and Stephanie Hoggert.

Contents

Foreword

MYTH reinvents the wheel. Cyclically. And, at each revolution, makes us believe we're seeing this old wheel for the first time. Myth holds this secret, without needing to hold it secret: its power is largely based on our deepest desires. We *want* to open the same gift over and over again. Like the "good sleep, bright fruit" of Wallace Stevens' "The Good Man Has No Shape," beautiful, wonderful, splendid gifts are rare. If, through myth's magic, we can be made to open gifts repeatedly, then blessings on the gifts of myth:

> To the left of the house of Hades
> under a graceful white cypress
> a well offers spring water.
> Don't drink there.
> —"Soul Ladder"

Myth will come out. This is its recurrent validity, its unchanging presence among us: that the more it changes, the more it remains the same, responding to primal urges, fears, and joys we all share.

When the translator's ear is attuned to essence instead of to syntax and surface only, translation becomes, automatically, mythic. Translation is, by its very nature, metamorphosis. Translation of mythic material is the literary locus where the Italian proverb *"traduttore, tradittore"* (translator, traitor) has least absolute veracity against the alchemical necessity by which the mind, in each new reincarnation, erupts its poetic lava from the universal molds.

Hogart's transmutations of the Orpheus literature achieves the crystalline lyricism of Mary Barnard's translations of Sappho, Robert Fitzgerald's Homer, or Robert Bly's Rilke. Hogart feels the myth, allows it to pass over him and through him. He makes of his English a compliant vessel, removing from it all that is not elemental: "Firstborn,/by your power/seed becomes/mighty tree" ("Proteus"). Hogart's versions turn arcane Gods into our household

familiars. He makes Orphic hymns as effectively spiritual today as
they were two millennia ago. From "Herakles":

> Shake the tree,
> give us a bite
> of golden apple
> for immortality.

In the most powerful pieces of this remarkable collection,
"Poseidon," "Mother of the Gods," "Kore," "Athene," "Melinoe,"
and "Dawn," Hogart reveals the technique by which he has freely
selected, plundered, rearranged and made his own: he is a latterday
priest of Orpheus, serving the spirit of music-inside-and-beyond-
words as Orpheus was priest to unknown Gods before him. Myth
holds the key to unlock Beowulf's "word-hoard"—as when, in the
hymn to "Apollo," Hogart pens:

> Strike summer's purest chord.
> Let the wind song
> of the syrinx sing
> a dance for Pan.

Whether the reader knows that "syrinx" is the voice box of a
singing bird, a nymph associated with Pan, and also the corridor of
an Egyptian pyramid leading to its hidden burial chamber, the word
works liquidly and alliteratively in the verse. On as many levels as
it can, or as few as it needs.

The impact of Hogart's investiture in the tradition he celebrates
is to make of these ancient, variously apocryphal prayers a new and
valid contemporary liturgy, with a rubric for every need and life-
event, from justice to dream, from sleep to happy hearth, from birth
to death:

> As soon as the spirit
> has left the sunlight
> then be wary of everything.
> —"Hammered in Gold"

By his free and idiosyncratic arrangement of the material related to the figure of Orpheus, Hogart reveals the mastery spoken of by T. S. Eliot: "Immature poets borrow. Mature poets steal." Like Hermes, thief and magus, Hogart steals the sacred secrets of Orphism to lay them at our feet. Truly hermetic presents, disguised as reverent lucidities.

Orphic initiates, Hogart points out, were spun on a wheel—until the yin and yang became amorphously, creatively, seamlessly unified gray. Happily, myth's wheel will not ever go away—whether the ceremonial wheel used by the Mayans and Aztecs with no knowledge of its utilitarian potential, or King Lear's metaphysically metaphorical plea to Cordelia (Act IV, Scene vii):

> You do me wrong to take me out o' the grave:
> Thou art a soul in bliss, but I am bound
> Upon a wheel of fire, that mine own tears
> Do scald like molten lead.

The eternal dance of Darkness and Light, black and white, chaos and order, pain and pleasure, birth and death, *anima* violence and *animus* escape, appears to be conflict only to those deprived of Orphic vision. To the initiates of Orpheus, conflict is cycle. Resolution is harmony, provided by music—from the cannibalistic chorus of Euripides' "The Bacchae" to the voracious fans of The Doors.

An invocation to this collection can conclude no better than to pray:

Enter here. Read. Enjoy. Abandon yourself. Allow yourself to be torn apart, then found—put back together on Hogart's word-created, world-creating, reinvented Orphic wheel.

—KENNETH ATCHITY

Boast all you want;
sell meatless food.
Call Orpheus lord.
Practice Bacchic rites
of ecstasy and revere
your windy scriptures.
I'm on to you.
I say to everyone:
beware these men.
They hunt their prey
with holy books
hiding shameful schemes.

—Euripides

After devoting his youth to education he learned stories about the
Gods. Then he went to Egypt, where he furthered his education and
became the greatest man among the Greeks, for his knowledge of
the Gods, and for his poems and songs. And because he so loved his
wife he dared the amazing deed of descending into Hades where he
enchanted Persephone with his song and convinced her to help him
bring his wife back to Earth.

—Apollonius of Rhodes

Orpheus with his lute made trees,
And the mountain-tops that freeze,
    Bow themselves when he did sing:
To his music plants and flowers
Ever sprung; as sun and showers
    There had made a lasting spring.

Everything that heard him play,
Even the billows of the sea,
    Hung their heads, and then lay by.
In sweet music is such art,
Killing care and grief of heart
    Fall asleep, or hearing die.

—Shakespeare

Honoring the Ancestors

I call these mutations because they are not exact translations.[1] The first seven poems are based on fragments found on small sheets of hammered gold buried with Orphic initiates in Crete and South Italy.[2] The rest are the Hymns of Orpheus, except for five interpolations of my own: "Magical Formula" based on two common Orphic sayings;[3] a hymn to Number to replace a lost hymn to Number; and hymns to Iakchos, Zagreus and Asteria.

These aren't really the *Hymns* of Orpheus. "Hymns" isn't the ideal word to translate the ancient Greek word *teletai*. Ritual, initiation, marriage, bearing fruit in season, ripening fruit to perfection, magical potency, and finishing are all related to *teletas*.[4]

These aren't really the Hymns of *Orpheus*.[5] Aristotle (350 B.C.) believed Orpheus never lived.[6] The eighteenth-century translator of Neoplatonism, Thomas Taylor, listed five men of the name Orpheus.[7]

W. K. C. Guthrie, author of the *Cambridge History of Greek Philosophy*, begins his book on Orpheus: " . . . *famous Orpheus*. In those words, torn from their context like so many fragments of ancient literature and embedded in the writings of a later author, Orpheus makes for us his earliest appearance in history."[8]

Orpheus may mean skillful.[9] Or "of the river bank,"[10] "orphan,"[11] "the dark,"[12] or "brownish red gray,"[13] possibly a reference to skin color. Historian Martin Bernal suggests *Orpheus* derives from Orpais, the ancient Greek transcription of the Egyptian word (ʾI)rpˤt, "hereditary prince."[14]

"Since I have mentioned Orpheus," the Sicilian historian Diodorus Siculus wrote during the reigns of the Caesars Julius and Augustus (30 B.C.), "I will say something about him. Dionysos gave gleaming-eyed Charops the kingdom of Thrace and the rites of Initiation. Oiagros inherited the kingdom and the rites and passed them onto his son Orpheus. Orpheus, by training and natural gifts, was exceptional; he made many changes in the rites. For this reason the Initiations that were given by Dionysos came to be called Orphic."[15]

Diodorus continues, "Orpheus is in culture, music and poetry easily the best of those we remember; he wrote astonishing, dulcet poetry. They said he could move trees and animals with his song. He studied long. He learned to understand the myths of religion. Then he lived in Egypt where he learned much more and so became the Greek expert on religion, ceremony, music, and poetry. He was an Argonaut. For love of his wife he descended into Hades where he so charmed Persephone with his music she agreed to help him bring his wife back; like another Dionysos, for they say Dionysos raised his mother Semele back to life from Hades."[16]

Around 1 A.D., the Greek historian and geographer Strabo, a doubter of religion and admirer of Rome, wrote: "Under Olympos is the city Dion. Near it is the village Pimpleia. They say Orpheus the Kikkonian lived there, a magician who at first was a wandering musician and a soothsayer and peddler of the rites of initiation. As time went on he thought more of himself and aimed at getting power with a revolutionary mob. Some welcomed him, but others, more suspicious, used guile and force to kill him."[17]

Konon, the myth collector of Cappadocia, wrote around 1 A.D.: "In the old days prophets played music . . . Orpheus, the son of Oiagros, and of the Muse Kalliope, was king of the Macedonians and Odyrsai. He was skilled in music, especially the lyre. Since Thracians and Macedonians love music, they favored him. He was torn to pieces by the women of Thrace and Macedonia because he would not let them join his rites. Or it may have been for another reason, for they say he hated women after the death of his wife. On certain days a crowd of armed Thracians and Macedonians would gather at Leibethra in a big temple. They would lay their weapons down before entering. The angry women took the swords. They killed anyone who tried to overpower them. They tore Orpheus to pieces and threw the pieces into the sea. They did not repent, so plague struck. An oracle told them to find the head of Orpheus and respectfully bury it. A fisherman finally showed it to them at the mouth of the river Meles. It was singing and had suffered no violence or decay; it was fresh and had the bloom of blood in it. They buried it under a great mound and fenced off the place. First a hero shrine, it grew into a temple. No woman may set foot in it."[18]

The Orpheus of myth was a Thracian musician. Most say he was the son of Apollo and beautiful voiced Kalliope, the Muse of Epic Poetry. A few say he was the grandfather of Homer. Thrace and Macedonia were the highlands of Ancient Greece. Thracians originated the worship of Ares, God of war, Artemis the quick-killing huntress, and Dionysos, God of wine. They wore their hair long and decorated themselves with extensive tattoos. They loved drinking, music, and dancing. They set out food for sea eagles. They bred, trained, and rode horses so well they are probably the source for the myth of the half-man, half-horse centaurs. Thracian women were fierce warriors, which may explain the legend of the Amazons.[19] Thracian men marched into battle drunk. Snowy Thrace was known as the Land of Prophets.[20]

Orpheus, unlike his Thracian kin, was gentle and contemplative. He fell in love with a beautiful virgin named Eurydice. On their wedding day a rapist chased her into the forest where she was fatally bitten by a snake. Orpheus mourned, singing songs so moving that animals, trees, and rocks wept and followed him. Orpheus mourned under the elms. His quiet music entranced lions and lynxes; deer danced, rocks and trees moved nearer to hear him, as in "A Tree Telling of Orpheus," the beautiful poem by Denise Levertov:

> Fire he sang,
> that trees fear, and I, a tree, rejoiced in its flames.
> New buds broke forth from me though it was full summer.
> As though his lyre (now I knew its name)
> were both frost and fire, its chords flamed
> up to the crown of me.

He descended into the underworld where Persephone, the Queen of the Dead, so loved his song she convinced her husband Hades to let Eurydice return to life. Hades had one condition: Orpheus had to trust him; he could not look back until Eurydice reached the sunlight.

Eurydice followed Orpheus through the underworld. He sang and played to her, resisting the urge to look back. The ghosts in the Fields of Joy turned from their pleasures. The ghosts in stinking, muddy Tartarus turned from their torments. All the underworld listened and watched in amazement. When Orpheus stepped into sunshine he turned to see his beloved but she had not yet reached the light. With a mournful cry, her ghost disappeared into darkness.

On a mountain top,[21] heartbroken Orpheus sang songs to the sun at dawn. The Thracian men left their wives to study with him. In revenge the women tore Orpheus apart. Or mad Maenads ritually executed Orpheus for tampering with the rites of Dionysos.[22] They tore his head off. Trees shed their leaves. The floating head, softly singing, passed weeping animals on a weeping river under a weeping sky. It floated to Lesbos, a large island in the Aegean Sea along the coast of Asia Minor. Lesbos, with high mountains and wide bays, exported corn, wine, and oil. Here Sappho invented lyric poetry and Terpander revolutionized music. At Lesbos, Apollo saved the head of Orpheus; its tomb became a famous Oracle of the Dead. The nightingales that nested there were said to sing especially sweet and loud.[23] After this, according to Plato, the spirit of Orpheus so despised women it sought rebirth as a motherless swan. A few later writers said Orpheus was struck by lightning for revealing the secrets of Zeus.

Orpheus the Thracian Poet is a character in what might be called the first novel, *The Argonautica* of Apollonius Rhodius (275 B.C.). Apollonius was a poet from Rhodes who became keeper of the Library at Alexandria. His Orpheus is one of the Argonauts, including Herakles and Jason, searching for the golden fleece. Orpheus plays to ease the rigors of rowing, he plays to calm the Argonaut Ida's drunken wrath, and silences the deadly Sirens with the beauty of his song. He sings an Orphic Rhapsody, a description of the creation of the world. In *The Orphic Argonautica* he is the lead character.[24]

Attic vase painters loved to portray Orpheus as a civilized Greek charming spear-wielding Thracian hillbillies in gaudy embroidered cloaks and pointy fox skin caps. Historians who believe Orpheus lived have offered various birth places for him: Thrace, Egypt,[25] Crete,[26] South Italy,[27] Persia,[28] India. The *-eus* ending indicates the name is from the most ancient Greek dialect (cf. Achilleus), predating Homer and the pantheon of Olympos, probably earlier than 700 B.C.[29]

The myth of the rape of Eurydice is most likely a mutation of the earlier myth of Persephone raped by Hades disguised as a snake.

The tragic tale of the backward glance is a late invention. In one variation of the myth Orpheus saves Eurydice. In the older versions, Eurydice is savage-eyed Agriope who saves Orpheus. On the earliest South Italian vases there is no Eurydice.[30] *Eurydike* is a title of the great Goddess that predates the pantheon of Olympos. Jane Harrison says the name means "Wide Ruling."[31] Others give "Universal Justice."[32] *Eur* has the connotation of wide, far reaching, universal. Like Kali of India, or the Egyptian lioness Goddess Sekhmet, the Goddess *Dike* (pronounced DEE-kay) was the ancient Greek personification of fate, justice, and order. Vase painters depicted her with a sword or hammer smiting *Adike*, Goddess of Injustice. Of course, Eurydice might be nothing more than a name, like Faith, Hope, or Charity.

Orphic religion inspired Pythagoras,[33] Plato,[34] Virgil,[35] Dante,[36] Blake[37] and Rilke. It lasted twelve centuries throughout the Mediterranean. South Italy, Sicily,[38] Crete, Athens (the first democracy in history),[39] Anatolia in Asia Minor,[40] Macedonia, and the Ciccone and Odrysai tribes of Thrace,[41] were its devotional centers. The Odrysai claimed him as an historical priest-king.[42]

Diodorus Siculus wrote: "Punishment in Hades of the unrighteous and Fields of Joy for the righteous were introduced by Orpheus, but were imitations of Egyptian funeral customs. The fabulous story of his visit to the underworld also came from Egypt." Herodotus, the father of history, is more succinct: "The rites called Orphic and Bacchic are really Egyptian and Pythagorean."[43]

There were no Orphic temples; an Orphic could worship any God. Pausanius the Lydian traveller, geographer and writer, reports that in his time (150 A.D.) many temples of Demeter were said to have been founded by Orpheus. Some have argued that the Hymns of Orpheus were the litany of the famous Eleusinian Mysteries, which honored Demeter's search for her abducted daughter Persephone.[44]

We don't know what took place in the Orphic rites.[45] Rumors abound. Initiates may have waited alone in rooms painted with scenes of death, disease, old age, poverty and war. Faces were dusted with chalk.[46] Rowdy celebrants were evicted by men called Horses.[47] Initiates were covered by a veil called a *synode*, a white sheet used for wrapping the dead.[48]

Some say at the center of the Orphic rites was a broad basket called a *liknon*. The Scholiast to Kallimachos wrote: "In the old days they lulled babies to sleep in *likna* for prosperity and health."[49] The fourth century A.D. grammarian Servius believed this was done immediately after birth. The *liknon* was used to winnow grain, to hold fruit and sacred objects; it was a cradle, a harvest basket and a cornucopia used in marriage rites.[50]

Important modern studies have argued that there never were Orphic rites; that Orphism was a purely literary tradition,[51] perhaps invented by Pythagoras or the Pythagoreans.[52] Some cite Plato and the famous Orphic quote "Nothing bitchier than a woman,"[53] to prove that Orphism was a male-only religious fraternity.[54] Still others say it was a loose confederation of frauds in white robes.[55]

As for the Hymns, they are probably not by Orpheus. Some scholars say they were written in the late Roman Imperial period (4th c. A.D.), probably in Asia Minor.[56] They do have a Neoplatonic flavor. Others, following Aristotle, say the ancient hymns were edited by a poet named Onomakritos who invented or reformed the Orphic mysteries in Athens around 500 B.C. The Greek grammarian of Constantinople Joannes Tzetzes (c. 1150 A.D.) claimed Onomakritos was one of those who arranged the books of Homer under Peisistratos.[57]

Peisistratos was a benevolent tyrant of Athens who protected small farmers. His ambitious building program included a majestic temple of Olympian Zeus. During his reign, Attic coin and black-figure pottery achieved prominence throughout the Greek world. After the death of Peisistratos, his eldest son Hippias ruled Athens. Poetry, sculpture, and architecture flourished under the patronage of Hipparchus, the younger brother of Hippias. Hipparchus encouraged the development of red-figure pottery. The Oxford Classical Dictionary says he was "frivolous and amorous."

Herodotus records that Hipparchus was a friend and patron to Onomakritos. A rival poet accused Onomakritos of adding an oracle to the Oracles of Musaios. Some believed Musaios was a great poet musician, high priest of the Mysteries of Demeter during the time of Herakles. Others believed he was the son of Orpheus.[58] Interpolating sacred oracles was an act of sacrilege. Hipparchus banished Onomakritos.

History loses track of Onomakritos at this point. Hipparchus was eventually assassinated. The Oxford Classical Dictionary hints: "Personal vices led to his murder." Hippias tightened his grip, but, beset by Persians to the north cutting off his gold supply in Thrace and Spartans attacking from the south, he fled Athens. He reappeared at the court of Xerxes. Hippias brought Onomakritos with him to read omens for the Great King of the Persian Empire.

By command of Hippias, Onomakritos was careful to read only the omens favorable for an invasion of Greece. Xerxes promised to restore Hippias to the throne. Old Hippias stood with Xerxes when the Spartan king Leonidas, three hundred of his guard, and five thousand Spartan Helots, Arcadians, Corinthians, Thespians, and Thebans held back a million Persians for three days at Thermopylae. Some historians say Hippias was killed when the Athenian fleet defeated Xerxes at Salamis. We know nothing of the fate of Onomakritos.[59]

Pausanias believed Onomakritos invented the myth central to Orphism.[60] The Titans cover their faces with chalk or quicklime (titanos: quicklime). They use toys to lure baby Dionysos away from the throne of Father Zeus. They tear Dionysos apart, cook and eat him. Athene alerts Zeus, whose lightning destroys the Titans. Athene saves the heart from which Dionysos is reborn. From the electrified fusion of the flesh of Dionysos and of the Titans, humanity is born.[61]

Every human is a confusion of Dionysos and Titan. The Dionysos part is immortal, beautiful, serene, wise, of the race of the stars.[62] The Titan part is mortal, anguished, rebellious, violent and deceitful. In two words: *soma sema*. The body, a tomb.[63] Forgetfulness is the Orphic evil, *lethe*.[64] Knowledge is memory and freedom. We live many lives purging the Titan.[65] From this point of view the Orphics taught catharsis through a course of abstinence and self-discipline similar to Jain yoga and the practices of the medieval Cathar sect that led to the Albigensian crusade.[66] They replaced drunken frenzy with rites of purification and spiritual enthusiasm and ecstasy, the Orphic *enthousiasmos* (to have a God within) and *ekstasis* (to stand outside oneself in trance).

Some scholars have argued that the Titan myth is a late addition to Orphism. The materials our knowledge of Orphism is based on are sparse and questionable: a few quotes, a few vases, some bits of gold, a few wall paintings. Opinions range from certainty that Orpheus was the writer of an Orphic Bible, the living founder of an ancient Greek religion of great importance—to doubt as to whether Orpheus was anything more than a garbled translation of Osiris or another foreign God disturbing pure Greek culture.[67]

Orpheus was called the Fisherman and the Good Shepherd; he was often depicted surrounded by peaceful animals.[68] Dionysos was called the Good Shepherd and the Bridegroom. Orpheus was supposed to have brought stone tablets down from a mountain.[69] Our Easter egg may be the Orphic egg.[70] Orphism influenced, paralleled, or borrowed from Christianity so profoundly that the nineteenth-century German scholar Dr. Eisler insisted Christianity stole the crucifixion from the wheel in the Orphic Mysteries.[71] Orphics were supposed to have been tied to the wheel so they could feel the dizzy helplessness of repeated reincarnation in forgetfulness.[72]

With the zealousness of a corporation eliminating its competition, the Church Fathers accused the Orphic mysteries of fornication and cannibalism.[73] We have evidence of a sacred marriage in the Orphic rites but the congregation respectfully dowsed their torches and waited in darkness for the announcement of the birth of the holy child. Orphism was a religion of moderation.

Accusations that live fawns or bulls were torn apart and eaten refer to the most primitive rites of Dionysos when, after dancing to frenzied flutes and cymbals, the Bakchoi would eat the sacrifice raw, then run bloody and screaming into the forest.[74] The Orphic rites rejected sacrifice.[75] "Orpheus taught men not to shed blood," Aristophanes wrote in The Frogs (3:393). Orphics believed that souls of animals evolve and become human, but human souls can regress and inhabit a cow, cat, dog, or any other animal.[76]

Orphics preached vegetarianism and non-violence.[77] No wool. No beans. Black and white beans were used for voting in ancient Greece, so "no beans" may mean stay out of politics. Retreat, contemplation, celibacy, a meatless diet, and ritual are given as methods of purification.

When Euripides warned against the "shameful schemes" of Orphism he blamed it for making its followers shy of war, civic discipline and business. Many frauds and cheats used Orphism to peddle false predictions and potions.

"Fake fortune tellers and healers," Plato wrote, "beseige the doors of rich men, they convince people they can purify sin in an atmosphere of feasting and pleasure. If a man wishes to harm an enemy, for a small fee it can be done with charms and binding spells, whether the man is just or wicked. They claim they can persuade the gods to do their will and call the poets as witnesses, even Hesiod and Homer . . . They show piled up books of Musaios and Orpheus, sons, they say, of the Moon and the Muses. With these recipes for sacrifice they convince individuals and cities that these rites, more like amusements that might please a child, can purify sins, even of the dead. They call them *teletai*, these ceremonies which free us from trouble after death; if we neglect them, they say, a terrible fate awaits us."[78]

Harrison compares God's breath on the waters in Genesis to a gateway painting at an ancient Orphic site: a winged white-haired old man named Light chases a blue-skinned woman named Dark Water.[79] But one is also reminded of old Brahma chasing his daughter Dawn in Hindu myth. The resemblance between Orphism and Hindu religion has led some to speculate that Orpheus was a wandering musician from India.

Joseph Campbell articulates the parallels in a paragraph thorny with Sanskrit: "a system both of thought and practice, exactly paralleling that of Indian asceticism, was communicated by initiated masters to little circles of devotees. The soul, it was declared, returned repeatedly to life, bound to the wheel of rebirth (compare the Sanskrit *samsara*). Through ascetism (Sanskrit, *tapas*), however, the body could be purged of its Titan dross (Sanskrit, *nirjara*, 'shedding') and the soul released (Sanskrit, *moksha*, 'release'). Also, rituals fostering meditation on the godly factor were of help (Sanskrit, *bhakti*, 'devotion'). And when, at last, in rapture (*samadhi*), the initiate cleaved to his own intrinsic being (*svasvarupam*), he was divine (*Shivaham*, 'I am Shiva.')"[80]

Was Orpheus a missionary from India? Campbell doubts it: "There have been those who sought to show that the movement stemmed from India, but the likelihood is not great. More likely is a common source in the archaic Bronze Age order, which in its last phases underwent the negative transformation that I have termed *The Great Reversal*, when a literature of lament arose from Egypt to Mesopotamia, following centuries of invasion, murder and rapine."[81]

In the fifteenth century A.D., Marsilio Ficino, under the patronage of Lorenzo the Magnificent, translated the Hymns with commentary and notes. He sang them privately and in public, accompanying himself on *lyra-da-braccio* in a mode appropriate to each God and Goddess. Carefully chosen color, hour, season, and incense, determined by Neoplatonic tradition, astrology and the law of correspondences, completed the ritual.[82] The philosopher Pico della Mirandola, Leonardo Da Vinci, and most of the great men of the Italian Renaissance, read Ficino's translation.[83] Shakespeare, Spenser, Purcell, Dowland, and other lights of the Elizabethan Renaissance were influenced by the Hymns, as were Voltaire, Diderot, and other *philosophes* of the Enlightenment.[84]

The Mysteries gave us civilization: dance, music, poetry, symposia and theater. As Jane Harrison wrote: "[In the Mysteries] we have all the apparatus of the stage, the appearances and disappearances, the dancing and the singing, the lights, the voices and the darkness. Religion gave all the circumstances and scenery, religion woke the instinct of intense impersonation, some genius made the dumb figures speak themselves and tragedy was born."[85]

Aristophanes joked that Orphics worshiped clouds, but the hymns are more like the Native American ritual of praising the beauty of the directions. The Gods of the Orphic hymns are aspects of a God. The Goddesses are aspects of a Goddess.[86] This God and Goddess are aspects of the One, as Plato called it. Orthodox rabbis would call it the unnameable YHVH. Catholics call it Godhead. Millions of Hindus call it Kali. The Sioux call it *wakan-tanka*, the

Great Spirit. It has a name in every language and dialect: a word for the mysterious source of consciousness, form, creativity and life. As Jane Harrison wrote: "We find ourselves at once in the atmosphere of mystical monotheism."[87]

—R. C. HOGART

The Hymns of Orpheus

Orphic Fragment

Exploding from the Great Soul,
souls reel and writhe,
seeking each other in space.

From planet to planet we fall,
crying for home in the abyss,
we are your tears, Dionysos.

Mighty one! God of Freedom!
Bring your children back into
your heart of singing light.

Soul Ladder

To the left of the house of Hades
under a graceful white cypress
a well offers spring water.
Don't drink there.

Find the well by the lake of memory.
Guardians protect the cold water.
Tell them:

    I am a child of earth
    and of starry heaven,
    but my race is of heaven.

    This you know.
    I am parched
    and perishing.

    Give me cold water
    from the lake of memory.

They will give you water
from the sacred spring
and you will live
a lord among heroes.

The Well of Memory

I am parched with thirst—
dying.

Drink from me, the eternal spring
on the right by the cypress.

Who are you?
Where are you from?

I am a child of earth
and starry heaven,
but my race is of heaven.

Hammered in Gold

As soon as the spirit
has left the sunlight
then be wary of everything.

Hail, you have suffered
the Suffering. This you
have never suffered before.

Once man
now God.

You are a kid
fallen in milk.

Hail, to you
walking on the right
by the sacred groves
and meadows of Persephone.

Charm

First born Earth,
counsel us.
All-mother,
sacred child
of the Mother,

all seeing Zeus,
Serapis, the sun,
far seeing fire,
maker of appearances;

Victory and Fortune,
Eros and the Fates,
preserve us, manifest
the spirit of healing.

Controller of everything,
you make thunder
and the sickle.

Save us from
noxious vapors
and tumors.

I will fast seven days.
In the night
and after daybreak.

Zeus, penetrator,
all seeing ruler
of every stream,

open the spring
of healing,
spare your drops of fire.

Cecilia's Golden Armor

She comes from the pure,
O pure Queen of the Dead.

Child of Zeus,
here is the armor
of memory:

a gift men love
to sing songs about.

For you, Cecilia Secundina,
to forever avert
the darkness of forgetfulness.

A Kid, I Have Fallen in Milk

Out of the pure I come.
Pure queen of the dead,
I am of your starry race.

I have paid the penalty
for unrighteous deeds.

Fate and the Immortals
struck me with lightning
thrown from the stars.

I have flown away
from the weary wheel
of sorrows. Queen,

with eager feet
I come to your circle
in the heart of the underworld.

I ask mercy
from Persephone,
that by her grace

she receive me
among the blessed
happy to find God in mortal.

Magical Formula

Mix honey with milk.
Drink it before sunrise
so you can have something
holy in your heart.

Remember—
many pretend;
few know.

Friend, Use it to Prosper

Hear this song.
Know a sacred way.

Thundering Zeus,
father of Gods,
mother Earth, shining sun,
splendid moon and starry night,

Poseidon, king of the poignant sea,
shadow haired Earth belter;
delicate Kore, Dawn in dark,
we honor you.

Arrow pouring Artemis;
blazing Apollo, sun beam archer
whose joy sings songs
of prophecy at Delphi;
intoxicating Dionysos,
we honor you.

Impulsive Ares,
quick to spill blood;
Hephaistos, lord of artistic fire;
great Aphrodite, risen from foam to light
and dark Hades, lord of shadows,
we honor you.

Hebe, giver of youth;
virile Herakles, master of work;
Artemis protector of birth,

opener of the gates to Earth,
we honor you.

Dike, mother of justice,
the noble God Piety,
brilliant Nymphs,
and musical Pan, lord of all,
we honor you.

Sacred Hera, queen of Gods,
beautiful Memory and pure Muses,
golden Leto, gentle Dione of Dodona,
clanging Kouretes, domestic Korybantes
and all children of Zeus,
we honor you.

Idaean Gods, the sky angel;
Agathodaimon, poppy in hand,
gentle spirit of good luck;
Themis of the prophetic eyes;
primordial Day and Night.
Faith and Fortune forever entwined,
we honor you.

Kronos, eater of children;
motherly Rhea; Thetis veiled
deep blue,
we honor you.

Okeanos, nymphs of the brine,
steady Atlas, shining Eternity
and endless Time, we honor you.

Splendid lake at the shore of death,
the Gods who rest beside it,
spirits good and bad,
irresistable Fate, we honor you.

Spirits of light and of fire,
of water, earth and shadow,
we honor you.

Leukothea, bright Dawn at sea,
amorous Semele,
mothers of great Dionysos,
we honor you.

Honey tongued Nike, drunk with success;
Asklepios, skillful healer who raised the dead;
dread Athene, master of war
who leaped full grown and armored
from the head of father Zeus,
we honor you.

Thunders and winds caged in mighty columns,
roaring in furious fight for release.
Attis, father of spring and immortal Adonis,
Beginning and End, we honor you.

We honor you all
and invite you
to a feast of love.

Hekate

Queen of blackest night,
we honor you.

Hekate, mother of magic,
at moonlit crossroads
you befriend the hopeless.

Torch held high
you walk beside Demeter
searching for Persephone.

You work from afar,
weaving spells of water
earth and sky you catch
every eye in a fatal trance.

Persian Artemis,
invincible huntress,
you hold freedom's key.

You rule over heaven,
earth and the sea.
You give wealth
and domestic blessings.

Each night drawn by bulls of mist
you shine light across the sky.
Full of your fire
crazed stags rattle antlers.

Ghosts and hounds follow you.
You are the black puppy
and the black she lamb.
We offer you eggs and fish.

Healer and guide,
give us pure desires.
Accept our love and bless us,
inspire awe in the dark.

Artemis, Opener of Gates

You can ease or sharpen
the pain of birth.

Women contracted on beds of strife
find relief in your mirror.

Gentle guardian of youth,
gracious mother,
compassionate and kind,

pleased by festival,
you part virgin lips.

You keep freedom's key
while we learn its use.

You love birth,
the playful crowd
of children,
cubs and flowers.

You surpass science and art
in the power of healing.

Merciful Artemis,
we honor you.
Care for us,
we are your children.

Night

Nyx, mother of sleep,
mother of Gods,
humans and animals,

star spangled Goddess,
at dusk your silence
calls dreams.

Pleased by lengthening shadows,
by exhaustion after feast,
friend to pleasure, heal us
with rest free from fear.

Dark stream, you drench the Earth.
Goddess of phantoms and shadows,
your drowsy power cleaves the day.

Ancient Night, black winged bird,
reveal your secrets.

Ouranos

Father of all,
source and end,
dance forever around
your Earth seed.

Gods and Goddesses
find their home in you.

Your watchful presence
cleaves eternity
with eternal laws.

Your great heart
wraps necessity
in soothing folds.

Spirit, matter—
indigo littered with stars—
amazing—.

Father of time,
divinity sublime,
shine.

We are dedicated seekers,
grace us with immortality.

Light

Amazing light, prince of the sky,
shining in starlight and moonglow,
blinding in sunshine, we honor you,
force that heals the world.

Your vivid blasts inspire life.
Purest element, burning power,
radiant star, dazzling flower,
hear us and give us peace.

Phanes the Revealer

Black winged Night
loved the wind.
A silver egg was born.

You burst from the egg.
Shining light
in four directions
you set the world whirling.

Mirror of yourself,
explorer of space,
you wear many shapes:

ram, snake, bull,
bright eyed lion,
your song fills space.

Father of Gods,
humans and animals,
first among the first,
we celebrate your power.

Mysterious blazing flower,
clear the darkness
from our eyes.

Radiant purity,
sanctify our lives
with infinite light.

Glory of the sky,
encircle the world
with your feathers.

Dark eyed splendor,
gentle and wise,
sacred beginning,
smile on our lives.

The Stars

Sky spirits
of purest light,
children of Night,
we honor you.

Dance circles
of far shining rays.

Eternal flames,
we are your sparks.
Light our way
through time.

The Sun

Titanic all seeing
golden eye
lighting our sky,
we honor you.

Reborn every instant,
your radiance delights us.

Lord of seasons,
your right hand gives dawn,
your left hand gives dusk.

Ancient sun, delicate and strong,
blazing across the sky,
scourge of evil, guide to goodness,

play your golden lyre,
light our world
with rays of harmony.

Bright eye soaring through the sky,
you rise and set in a nest of color,
your heat gives life.

Stream lover, world master,
father of Justice supreme,
faithful defender, eye of right,

light of life, crack your whip
and guide your fiery horses.

The Moon

Goddess of silver light,
bull horned searcher
through gloomy night,
we honor you.

Stars attend your orbit
as you glide
a torch in the sky.

Blue rays shine from you.
Your amber body
reflects noon into night.

All seeing eye
decorated with stars,
favor the watchful
and prevent strife.

Grace us with
intuition's light.

Beautiful lamp,
ornament
and friend of night,
your phases guide life.

Queen of stars,
brilliant Artemis,
veiled in night,

moon lamp of purest light,
shine your gentle rays.
Accept with pleasure
our humble praise.

Nature

Ancient mother,
holy artist,
queen of constantly
unfolding creation,
we honor you.

Untamed all-tamer,
eternally splendid,
bright serenity,
first born.

Lady of the shining stars
dancing breathless circles,
gem of divine powers,

finite, infinite,
known, all knowing
yet secret within us,
you invoke yourself.

Lead us, mother of life,
give us wisdom,
grace us with beauty.

You are justice
supremely strong
ruling every chaos.

You are spiritual and earthly,
a friend to piety,
sweet to goodness
and bitter to evil.

You are the most powerful;
you nourish all.

Your pure mind full of seeds
gives crowds of stars and flowers
creating worlds streaming
to receding horizons.

Your hand holds up space.
You direct the wind.
You hinge the world
with the bolt of force.

Courageous, fatal,
all conquering queen,
hear our song.

Care for us.
Grant plenty,
adventure and comfort,
constant peace and health.

Pan

Great Pan, God of the wild,
we honor you, ruler of sky,
sea and earth, Light
ensouling all.

The world is yours.
Every thing reflects you.

Delighted by shady groves,
dancer under the stars,
you rule the seasons.

Pan, shepherd of goats,
giver of milk, meat and skin,
your horns sprouted
and the world began.

Inspire us
with dance and song.
Protect us from fear.

You love the hunt,
Echo's solitary song
and playful nymphs.

All your works
reach fruition.
You rule increase.

Pan, splendid as cloudless sky,
sweet as fruit,
obscure as the deepest cave,
subtle as a snake,

wise as a wolf,
no man can resist
your panic.

You hold up the Earth.
You rule the restless sea,
even ancient Ocean, Earth hugger,
loves your law.

Air nourishes fire,
fire inspires life,
even the shining blue sky
loves your law.

Protect and care for
matter dancing everywhere.
Grace us.

Lift us, mighty Pan,
come near, excite us.
Give us creative power
and freedom from fear.

Herakles

Secret friend,
prophet and champion,
lord of time,
great archer,

glorious gift of Hera,
compassionate lord
of creative power,
frighten away our fears.

You are Earth's
most beautiful flower.

Serenely enjoying
all work
you never weary.

You capture the lion.
You kill the hydra
that grows back two heads
where one is cut off.

You catch the wildest stag
and the strongest boar.
You fight the centaurs.

You bend rivers
to clean stables.
You shoot birds
that steal food.

You herd cattle.
You wrestle giants.
You capture the bull
and the wild horse.

The queen of the Amazons
smiled when she
gave you her sash.

You fetched the vicious
three headed dog Cerberus
from the underworld.

The first fire
shines in you.
Your strong heart
has a thousand names.

We honor you.
Save us from disease
and injury. Heal us.
Drive away disaster.

Shake the tree,
give us a bite
of golden apple
for immortality.

Kronos

Father of Titans,
great spirit
of Gods, humans
and animals,

we honor you,
wise, pure, strong
ruler of the waves.

Flowing forms
in their hourly deaths
learn your power
that molds the world.

Father of Time,
divine Kronos,
you speak a million tongues.

Flower of Earth,
star of the sky,

lover of Rhea,
ancient root of all,
nothing can resist you.

Present everywhere
you know all secrets.

We honor you,
give blameless life
and easy death.

Rhea

Daughter of first born Eros,
illustrious Rhea, hear us,
we honor you.

With terrible strength
you guide your chariot
drawn by charging lions.

Mother of Zeus,
whose powerful hands
throw thunderbolts.

You love the fury
of pounding drums,
clashing shields,
blaring trumpets.

You love battles
and the horrid howling of men.
Mother of war,
deceitful savior,

liberate us.
Mother of the Earth,
of Gods, mortals
and mountains,

mother of the spacious heavens,
of winds and the wide spreading sea.
Drive disease forever away.
Grace us with peaceful abundance.

Zeus

You were.
You are.
You will always be

supremely sacred Zeus,
we dedicate this rite to you.

Under the oak of Dodona
your prophet priests
with unwashed feet
crouch on the ground

listening to your voice
speaking softly in rustling
leaves and cooing doves.

You simply wish
and things come true.

You are thunder.
You are bright day,
rain, wind and dew.

Mother Earth,
her towering mountains,
the roaring sea,
you are father of us all.

You are law,
civil rights,
privacy and property.

You are landmarks
and boundaries.
Protect sweet marriage.

Show mercy to the unfaithful.
Punish perjury.
Judge the dead.

Show mercy to conscience
stricken outcasts.
Civilize us.

Grace us with love,
power, wisdom, peace,
health and wealth.

Hera

Royal Hera,
majestic queen,
we honor you.

Virgin, mother, crone,
shield sweet marriage,
console the divorced,

ease the pangs of birth,
protect our children.

Enthroned in the blue
heart of the sky
watch over us.

Mother of rain,
the peacock
and the cuckoo,

you guide the universe
from blasting winds
and swelling seas
to rolling rivers.

You give us
ox and yoke,
gentle cows
with luminous eyes,

and plump ears of corn
golden in green fields.
We celebrate your festival
of flowers in spring.

Hear us, blessed Goddess,
beloved wife sister of Zeus,
Goddess of the moon and stars,
shine joy and peace upon us.

Poseidon

King of the poignant sea,
your powerful arms
belt the world,
we honor you.

You are indigo calm
deep
beneath stormy sea.

The tides obey
your bronze trident.
From your black curls
slide great waves.

Your sea horses
gallop in tidal waves
and trickling foam.

You are the dolphin,
and the palm tree.
You are the healthy
salt air of the sea.

Your thunder voice
enrages the deep as you
ride the boiling ocean
waves crashing at your command.

You are the black bull
drowning in the river.
You gave us horses.

Night haired Earth shaker,
survey Ocean's play
with a contented smile.

Split open rocks
and reveal fresh water
fountains and springs.

Make firm our roots in Earth.
Send prosperous winds.
Give us peace and health.
Pour blessings in shining waves.

Hades

Remote from sight,
forever sunk in night,
your gloomy realm
underlies solid earth.

Subterranean Zeus,
Dionysos, we honor you.

Your key unlocks
the secret gate.
Your seasonal gifts
nourish and enrich us.

You are the basis
of Gods and humans.

In the dismal plain that stretches
from horizonless darkness to the same,
where breathless specters roam
seeking light in dark dreams,

there you reign:
in the dust on the turtle's back,
in the rushing dark river
where Earth binds her roots to Fate.

Mighty one, your dread wisdom
determines our way at death.
You carry us from the grassy plains
down to your pit of shadow.

Driven by love you fly
to the city of mystery
and in the deepest cave there,
in the cave of Night, you hide us.

Commander of works seen and unseen,
omnipotent glory bright,
sacred songs delight you,
smile on us.

Thundering Zeus

Father Zeus, you blind and deafen us
when you shake the Earth
and rip the sky with lightning.

You thunder and Olympos shakes.
You shroud flames in clouds.

Our hearts beat wild with fright,
our hair stands when you arrive,
you are omnipotent pure life.

With your eternal roar
you devour all.

Wild and terrible,
you roll flame
in quick bolts
like roots of fire.

The sky flashes.
The bright sea boils.
Every creature shivers.

Blessed Zeus, we honor you.
Your wrath explodes the deep,
flooding darkness with light.

Let us see your fire on our peaks.
Don't restrain your strength.
Grace us with immortal memory,
health, wisdom and peace.

The Father of Lightning

Zeus, the power
of your light thunders.

The flowing fire
of your voice

flashes through
lucid clouds.

God of wild power,
we honor you.

Grant a good life
and noble death.

Clouds

Mothers of rain
traveling over
heaven's plain,
nourish our crops.

Wind driven
water bellies,
we honor you.

Thundering lions
of fleece,
flash fire.

Floating river
encircling the Earth,
we sing to you.

Pour sweet rain
on thirsty soil.

Tethys

Blue eyed queen,
dancer in the deep,
when you smile

winds rise
to wash the beach
with gentle waves.

When you frown
tidal waves crash
against continents.

Playing in the quiet sea
you love to watch our
passing sails.

Mother of Aphrodite,
mother of animals,
give fresh water springs,
cool clouds and rain.

We honor you, Tethys,
care for us.
Float us safely
over stormy seas.

Nereus

Ocean root,
we honor you.

Fifty beautiful mermaids
swim gracefully
beside your blue chariot
in dark rippled sea.

From Ocean's inky throne
you rule the limits of Earth.
When you boil the sea
Earth shakes her back of plates.

Hear us, Nereus,
don't make the Earth dance.
Grace us with tranquil health,
wisdom and peaceful wealth.

Proteus

You hold the key
that unlocks the deep.

Firstborn,
by your power
seed becomes
mighty tree.

Changing intricate matter
you elaborate life
into endless shapes.

Your logic is everywhere
in everything.

You are the essence
and principle of form.

We honor you, Proteus.
Grant happiness,
prosperity,
a good death.

Earth

Gaia, mother of Gods
heroes and mortals,
prolific destroyer,
parent of all you devour,
we honor you.

You give us fruit,
herbs and flowers.
You are the pure pulse
in everything.

You give birth everywhere
yet you are forever virgin.
Immortal crowned with grace,
mother of the children of time,

you love sweet smelling
grassy plains drenched in rain.

Blossoming spirit,
great heart of our world,
the music of the spheres
guides you through space.

Smile on this little song,
mother of us all.
Make our fruit sweet.
Make our water sweet.
Make our hearts sweet as yours.

The Mother of the Gods

Virgin, mother, nurse,
whore and crone,
we honor you.

Lioness, you destroy
the pride of bulls.
You are the axis.

You are the heart
enthroned in every being.

Your love protects us.
You feed and care for us.
You guide the seasons.

Gods and mortals
flow from you
like seas and rivers.

Mother of goodness and bounty,
we rejoice in your gifts,
amazed by your kindness.

You tame every wilderness
and make wild every street.

We pound the drum for you,
mighty queen. Celestial,
primal, you give life,
sustain it and take it.

Help us, wife of Time,
we are your incense.

Hermes

Angel of Zeus,
son of Maia,
you judge
every competition.

Good shepherd,
priest and sage,
celestial messenger
of a thousand skills,

you lulled and killed
hundred eyed Argos
to give the peacock
gorgeous feathers.

Gracious prophet,
guide and guardian,
you love gymnastics,
secrets and tricks.

Giver of good things,
ready helper,
your gifts are
casually found treasures.

You give gain,
honest or dishonest.
Doorways, roads
and borders amuse you.

Wings on your feet
you soar through space
singing all music
in every language.

With a touch
of your wand
you bring sleep,
a dream or death.

We honor you, Hermes,
help us in our work.
Give us eloquent speech
and eager virility.

Give us our necessities
and sharp memory.
Give us good luck.
Close our lives in peace.

Kore

Black Mother Night,
your children are
Sleep, Love, Dreams,
the Fates, Nemesis,
Old Age and Death.

You dwell deep in Earth
beyond the dismal gates
that separate
the living from the dead.

Golden daughter of Demeter
and Zeus, wife of Hades,
beautiful avenger,
mother of the Furies,
mother of Dionysos,

you were a virgin
walking in a field
when Hades saw you
and took you away
in his black chariot.

Your mother searched
everywhere for you.
She found you
in the underworld.

Persephone,
because you ate
pomegranate seeds
at the table of Hades

Zeus decreed
you spend six months
every year underground.
We call it winter.

When you return
to wander smiling
in fields of sweet grass
your footsteps and voice
awaken spring.

We know you in
bursting pomegranates,
laughing children
and nodding flowers:

roses, violets, crocuses,
irises, hyacinths, anemones,
daughters of the wind.

Under the black poplar
and white willow
you whisper secrets

of shade without sound
and coming out to light.

Persephone
of the beautiful ankles
and aspen hair,

you are the star
in the apple.

Autumn wed
giver of life and death,
we honor you.

Give us rich increase,
healthy crops
and precious peace.

From your gentle hand
let fall health and joy.

Free us from bleak strife.
When we stand before death
send us willing to the essence
from which we came.

Welcome us
in your splendid palace.
Let us play
in your beautiful fields.

Dionysos

You sleep in Persephone's hall.
Seasons turn.
You lull to sleep
and wake the years.

God of inspiration,
thrice born king
mingled of mortal
and immortal seed,

God of the wilderness,
secret as deep caverns,
sweet voiced, pure hearted
warrior strong as a bull,

father of the vine,
you who gave us wine,
give us wisdom
and peace divine.

Grapes and ivy mingle
in your wine red hair.
Dionysos, we honor you,
son of Zeus and Kore,

born in mystery,
hear our plea:
give us joy
and blameless plenty.

The Kouretes

Flyers in time
with the ringing lyre,
dance to protect
baby Dionysos.

Dread lords,
armored defenders,
givers of prosperity,
guards of Queen Kore,

protect our holy rite.
Courageous Kouretes,
we honor you.
Defend us from strife.

Athene

Fully armored you leap
from the womb
in the head of Zeus.

He trusts you
with the aegis
of omnipotence.

Illustrious warrior,
principle of wisdom,
we honor you.

Teach us diplomacy
and strategy.
Give us foresight.

You invent the plow.
You give practiced hands
to build strong ships.

You teach us
to spin and weave,
make shoes, work gold.

You invent the flute
and inspire its music.

You love mountains,
the brilliant peaks
and shady groves.

In the gloom you walk,
fierce gray eyes
piercing the dark.

You are the owl,
the rooster, the snake
and the spider.

Mistress of every art,
master of war,
inspired prophetess,

Athene the grinder,
dance the war dance,
shake your spear,

rage against injustice.
Inspire us with the prowess
of righteous fury.

Give us your mirror,
balance and sword
so we can slay the Gorgon.

You who trampled down
the flaming Titans,
purge the evil threatening us.

We pray day and night:
let your beauty
and omniscience shine.

You give bunches of figs
and the glittering
dew that nourishes
fields and meadows.

You taught us
to tame and bridle
wild horses.

You gave Athens
her olive trees
and the golden words
that gilded Greece.

Give us peace and health,
wisdom, happiness and wealth,
ever present, be our guide.

Grant us strength and wit,
teach us the craft
of giving the dying life.

Nike

Omnipotent Nike,
desired by everyone,
we honor you.

Beat your wings
against injustice.
Conquer war and rape.

Confer the battle trophy,
the victor's wreath,
the mark of sweet renown.

You rule everything.
End our strife
with cries of Victory.

Protect us.
Give us eyes
blazing conquest.

Guide us
to illustrious deeds
and immortal fame.

Leto

Gentle queen of night,
mother of dancing lights,
veiled Leto, we honor you.

Pregnant with immortal twins
you fled the wrath of Hera.
For you Zeus fixed

floating Ortygia,
island of the quail,
to the bottom of the sea.

Under the watchful gaze
of your sister Asteria,
by the rushing stream
and the sacred pool,

in the shade of palm and laurel,
you gave birth
to twins of light:

Apollo, lord of the shining
peaks of Delos,
and Artemis of the rushing arrows.

Bless us, Leto;
complete our song
with your smile.

Asteria

Deathless mother of Hekate,
to refuse amorous Zeus
you threw yourself
like a meteor
into the boiling sea.

You became Ortygia,
land of the quail,
where your sister Leto
bore Artemis and Apollo,
twin lamps of the sky.

The glory of your light
shines through endless space.
The infinite eyes of night
dance serene spirals
singing you songs of praise.

Star Goddess, we honor you,
brighten your light within us.

Apollo

Blessed singer,
smile on this song.

Illustrious power,
rape avenger,
God of shining health,
evergreen of wealth,
play your golden lyre.

Dragon slayer,
father of oracles,
archer with arrows of light,
sun prince of Muses,
drive away all diseases.

Golden haired wonder,
you see all within
and all beneath the sky.
Your omens guide us
to purity and goodness.

You watch ceaseless light
and the mysteries of Earth.
Your keen eyes pierce
silent night.

You are the root
of stars and space.
You inspire Nature's music
with your ringing lyre.

Seeds, plows,
flourishing fields
glistening at dawn,
belong to you.

You are dolphin,
bay and laurel.
You are palm tree,
swan and hawk.

You are mouse and snake.
You are wolf and deer.
You are crow, raven,
grasshopper and griffin.

Always everywhere
you give subtle advice
through oracles, dreams,
and bird flight.

Teach us the science
of harmonies and limits.
Tune winter's deep string
to spring's sweetness.

Strike summer's purest chord.
Let the wind song
of the syrinx sing
a dance for Pan.

Keeper of the seal
that stamps the world with forms,
hear our song
and save us.

Artemis

Ease the pain
of our labor.

Smooth the creases
worry folds
in our faces.

Splendid with starlight
your keen eyes
seek and destroy
the antlered stag.

You love deep forest,
subtle trails,
yelping dogs
and wooded peaks.

You are the moon
roaming the wilds.
You are the cedar
and the walnut tree.

You give sweet water,
rivers and springs.

Girls with pine torches
dance around laurel trees,

lady of the lake,
we honor you,
purify us,
save us from all evil.

Most beautiful Artemis
of the dancing plants,
mother of bees, boars, and bears,

we spin a wheel
of torches for you,
we offer
two jars of fish.

Give us peace, health,
strength and wealth.
Give us the skill
of the hunter.

The Titans

Mighty children of sky and Earth,
illustrious sparks of Tartarus,
fountains and elements
of affliction,
we honor you.

You are the butchers
who feasted on Zagreus.
Every creature
wears your ashes.

Cool your rage.
Rise gently
from darkness
to sweet light.
Give us peace.

The Kouretes

Bronze clashing
priests of Ares
in your bodies
of sky, earth and sea,
we honor you.

You breathe
and all animals
come to birth.
You gave us
mystic rites.

Raining wind
and thunder in the sky
you bend stubborn oaks.
Animals flee your storm.

Whirled by you,
oceans crash
against shores.

We drown in your storm.
Replenish us
with a balmy breeze.

Soldiers of Rhea,
run circles
to flute and drum.

Clouds rise from
your dancing feet
to cool the desert.

Rainbows of flowers
rise from your steps.
The immortal spirits who nourish
and destroy us obey you.

Guardians of infant Zeus,
keep us
in the din
of your protection.

Korybas

Ruler of the whirling Earth,
we never see you
you so love Night.

In the shade of the desert
blood spills;
the gentle purity of Earth
transforms into a dragon.

Rest your anger,
we honor you.
Drive our fears away.

Give us strength
to purge the Titan.

Demeter

Pure mother bee,
giver of wealth,
generous nurse,
lover of peace,

nourish the corn.
Give us seeds and fruit.
Watch over the harvest
and the threshing.

You dwell in the solitude
of the valley of Eleusis.
Your gentle wisdom
first yoked ox to plow.

Give us sustenance.
Green of every leaf,
lucid, earthly and pure,
give us bliss.

Every winter you search
for your daughter Kore;
two torches held high
in a dragon drawn chariot.

The rainbow brood
of flowers and fruit
belong to you,
mother of summer.

Give us peace,
wisdom, health,
fair concord
and blameless wealth.

The Mother

Far traveling
mother of Gods and mortals
by grief oppressed,
you found rest in Eleusis.

Dionysos walks ahead,
showing you the way.

By grief oppressed,
draped in black,
mourning for Kore,
you let no seed sprout
from dead Earth.

We honor you,
famous Demeter,
bless us.

Mise

Law giver, seed giver
of a thousand names,
we honor you.
Dip your sceptre of leaves
in our spiraling incense.

You delight in
your mother's rites
in elegant Eleusis
and wild Phrygia,
in pleasant Cyprus

on fertile plains
by the flooding Nile
where your mother
dark Isis reigns.

Inspiration of makers,
save us.
Protect us from hate.

The Seasons

Daughters of Themis
and all father Zeus,
we honor you.

You are justice, peace and law.
You inspire green spring
and hillsides of flowers,

flourishing color
decorates air with dew.

You ripen crops,
you bring rain,
hail and snow.

You attend Kore as she rises
from shadow when the Fates
and Graces lead her into the light.

With triumphant Demeter
and smiling Zeus,
bless us.

Give us bounty.
Give us beauty.
Give us grace.

Semele

Your shining hair
lights the night,
mother of Dionysos,
we honor you.

Zeus loved you
and granted you
any wish. You asked
to see his splendor.

You were vaporized
by the roaring sun
of his unveiled glory.

Kore lets you visit
mortals in the night.
You love to attend
the sacred rites

when singers tell
your son's bright birth,
celebrating secrets
of purity and mercy.

Daughter of time
and the sky,
grace us with serenity.

Thundering Dionysos

Universal God
of many names,
Son of Lightning,
strength of the bull,

you love the cries,
swords and blood
of furious battle.
Remember peace.

Minotaur killer
Theseus deserted
Ariadne Aphrodite;
she cried on the beach.

Love found her
on the island
where you crowned
her with stars.

Dionysos,
God among us,
we honor you.
Inspire us.

Dionysos in the Basket

Joy of flowers
tended by sweet nurses,
Maenads and Muses—
Aphrodite's fairest petal,

your smile drives
Nymphs mad with
laughter and dancing
in the wilderness.

Looking into your eyes,
son of Zeus and Kore,
even Gods know awe.

New born bunch
of purple grapes
in a cradle,
we honor you.

Dionysos, Pillar of Light

You give grape seeds
power to break dirt.
You ripen to bleed
on the wine press.

When lightning and thunder
quake mountains,
twine your vines
around our pillars.

Mighty Dionysos,
make our house strong
as you did for Kadmos
father of writing.

Sabazios

Illustrious father,
child of mighty Kronos,
we honor you.

You hid Dionysos
in your thigh.
Protect us.

Iakchos

Baby Dionysos,
with your mouth
full of milk,

savior of poets,
inspire us.

Reveal your secrets.
Give us clear vision
and accurate memory.

Touch and deepen
music in words.

Zagreus

Zeus as a snake
coiled and licked
Persephone pregnant.
You were born.

Son of God,
happy child,
your innocent play
is perfect ritual.

Thunder and lightning
are your toys.

Little Dionysos,
teach us ways
to earn the grace
and wisdom of the Gods.

Hipta

Nurse of Dionysos,
mother of secret rites
choruses sing
by crackling fires,

you saw the Titans
butcher Zagreus.
They boiled then
roasted him.

Zeus blasted them
with lightning.
From the bloody ashes
humans were born.

When we hunger
for raw flesh,
blood drenched bronze,
frenzied women,

sweet nurse who
witnessed our birth,
protect us.

Dionysos

Father Zeus hid
your beating heart
in his thigh.

With golden pins
he knit his skin
to keep you safe.

You were born.
You died. You
were born again.

You nourish our crops.
You raise seeds
to flourishing beauty.

You are tigers, bears,
dolphins, panthers, lions,
goats, snakes and braying asses.

Your healing flowers
and wine refresh
the weary worker.

For you women
in fawnskins dance
singing on mountains.

Dionysos of the trees,
raise your reed
with its pine cone tip

and hidden spear point
trailing grapes, vines,
ivy leaves and berries.

God of mount Nysa,
where pine and cinnamon
perfume the breeze,

save us.

The Nymphs

Children of Ocean,
dwellers in the dark
wet recesses of Earth,
we honor you.

Nurses of Dionysos,
as golden bees
you nourish
flowers and fruit.

You live in meadows,
in caves so deep
they reach the core
yet you fly like a bird.

You tend fountains,
meandering streams
and morning dew.

You love to wander
dancing with Pan
through remote valleys
thick with flowers

to mountain peaks
where you share
elation.

Inspiring singers,
white robes
streaming perfume,

you refresh
the green glow
of the forest.

You love wolves
and lions as much
as pastured goats
and cattle.

You love ice,
the sea
and oak trees.

Favor us with ample seasons,
wealth and lasting health.

Dionysos, Soul of the Sun

You begin all ceremonies.

Dionysos,
child of the primal fire,
we honor you.

You are the eye of Kore
watching us.

Howler, warrior,
fountain of light,

firstborn of our family,
secret flower of Zeus,
lead the dance and choir.

Golden haired Apollo,
ripen our vines.

Dionysos

Wake,
sleeper in Persephone's hall.

Wake
for the sacred feast.

Wake
the nymphs sleeping at your feet.

They will dance and sing,
wild with the joy of life.

Wake,
Dionysos who gave us the vine.

Accept our incense.
Care for us.

Silenus, the Maenads and the Satyrs

Vigilant Silenus,
we honor you.

Father of lawful rites,
lord of streams,
open the wine skin
of accurate prophecy.

Forever young Maenads,
first priestesses
of Dionysos,
we honor you.

Satyrs,
spirits of the wild,
we honor you.

Bless our incense
and wake Dionysos;
teach him his dance.

Inspire our celebration
to shine through the night,
bless our sacred rite.

Aphrodite

Child of Ocean,
amazing beauty,
we honor you.

You rule deep earth,
encircling heaven,
the stormy seas
and everything in them.

Mother of sweet marriage,
you join the world together
with laughter and harmony;
even the Fates obey you.

Every eye seeks you.
Give us beauty and love.

Delighted by secrets
and lavish feasts
you are concord
and persuasion.

You are beautiful necessity
even in the frenzy of the shark.
Delicate as sea foam of Cyprus,
fragrant as Syrian oils,

bright as golden chariots
on Egyptian plains
by the sandy bank
of the turquoise Nile,

a choir of the loveliest Nymphs
sings a hymn to your beauty.

With reverence we ask
for the gift of grace.

Adonis

You stand in the desert,
illustrious spirit
with shining hair.

You nourish everything.
You are more beautiful
than male or female.

Doomed to set,
you rise in glory.
Laughter follows tears.

Graceful power,
flower of love,
we honor you.

Son of dark Hades
and bright Persephone,
you light the sky.

Smile on us.
Protect us.
Care for us.

Hermes Psychopomp

Servant of the Fates,
guide us on the path
to the other world.

Son of Dionysos
and Aphrodite,
guide us to Persephone.

You lead the wretched,
sodden with mud,
into long rest in the dark.

A touch of your wand
brings sleep
or wakes the dead.

Guide of souls
forever flowing
to the other side,

we honor you
Hermes,
guide us.

Love

Holy and pure source
of sweet delight,
we honor you.

Impetuous fire,
with arrows
of fierce desire
you pierce even Gods.

You play everywhere,
curious and cautious.
You hold the keys
to heaven and Earth.

From fertile plains
and far spreading sea
to caverns underground,
everything obeys you.

You are the only
ruler of the universe.

The Fates

Deep in the dark
of the deepest cave
a fountain streams
through barren rock.

It travels far
to feed the lake
you sit beside,
daughters of Black Night.

You have power
over all.

Elated men, who forget
they are born to decay,
ride the fatal plain
with opinion for a guide

while you keep secret
the limits of hope.
In dark purple
inaccessible

perfect justice
waits to demonstrate
the immense power
of Law.

Daughters of Necessity,
you see everything.
You are the eyes
of all knowing Zeus.

Klotho spins the thread.
Lachesis measures it.
Atropos cuts it.

Sisters of Death,
protect us.

The Graces

Radiant Aglaia,
flowering Thaleia
and joyous Euphrosyne,
we honor you.

Graces, forever fair,
give us pleasure,
delight and beauty.

Nemesis

You see everything.
You alone rejoice
at the sight
of perfect Justice.

You see our thoughts
rolling without rest
and you change them.

Everyone knows you.
Men everywhere
groan under the burden
of your judgment.

Your calm gaze
constantly searches
our dark places.

Guide our lives.
Show us mercy
when we are in need.

With good advice
and freedom from arrogance
strengthen reason everywhere.

Justice

Piercing eye of Zeus,
you see everything.

You punish the wicked.
You avenge cruelty.

No deed escapes
your bright gaze.

You bring opposites together
in the equality of truth.

You avenge the havoc
of persuasive bad advice.

You avenge every crime
of passion or greed.

You favor the just
and hinder the wicked.

Stand beside us
when we die.

Inspire and witness
a blameless life.

Equality

Eternal friend
of humanity,
we honor you.

Essence of harmony,
friendship and peace,
perfect the other virtues.

Law

King of Gods and men,
celestial Law,
we honor you.

You are the pattern
of all patterns,
Nature's firm foundation.

Harmony of the stars,
give us
laws forever just.
Defend us.

You break men
who challenge you.
Grant a noble end
to a good life.

May our eyes
always gaze upon you
as we walk
a path of Justice.

Number

You describe
and analyze.

Teach us secrets
of music and measure,
architecture of harmony.

You are Fair Order
of our universe,
our grammar and logic.

You are ratio,
rank, proportion,
perspective, division,

multiplication,
subtraction
and addition:

the One becomes many,
the many become One.

Ares

You love raining torches
and bloody battlefields.

The stink of human gore
is your favorite incense.

You love the din of war:
crashing swords and spears,

screams of hatred,
rage and pain.

You embitter human life
with works of woe.

Fear and Panic
are your children.

You reduce cities
to smoking ruins.

You are the dog
and the vulture.

You are the boar
who gores Adonis.

Listen to Aphrodite.
Hear Dionysos.

Let Demeter keep
your iron sword.

God of war,
protect innocence.
Give us peaceful
gentle abundance.

Hephaistos

Your hammer and pincers
master every art.
Molten bronze and gold
flow from your workshop.

Volcanoes, lava,
flame from Earth,
pure clear light
of the shining sun,

that is all
we see of you.
You are the heat
and strength of fire.

Father of tribes,
builder of shelter,
inventor of cities,
we honor you.

Our strong bodies
are your handiwork.
Breathe upon us
an even flame.

Asklepios

You grant the art of healing.
You give medicine.
Kind physician,
we honor you.

Grace us
with good health.

Ease our pains.
Restrain pestilence.
Quench raging disease.

Apollo's honored son,
constant warrior
against sickness,

husband of the Goddess
with shining hair:
healthy Hygieia;

saviour,
defend life,
ease death.

The Furies

Daughters of Earth and shadow,
children of Black Night,
dread Goddesses,
we honor you.

Tisiphone, avenger of blood,
mother of retaliation;
Allekto the pain inflictor
we fear to name;

terrifying Megaira
mother of crisis,
mother of grudges,
we honor you.

You see inside us.
You judge.
You take away peace of mind
allowing no rest for the wicked.

Children who fail
their duty to their parents.
Parents who fail
their duty to their children.

No one escapes you.
You punish the liar.
You punish the miser
who refuses a beggar.

The son who kills his mother
never washes the blood away.
You are the mother's curse,
the miasma of bad luck

that infects him
and anyone who helps him.
You wait for him
in darkness by Styx.

Invisible,
quick as thought
you fly to avenge
every injustice.

Dog headed, snake headed,
draped in gray,
your red eyes search
the newly dead.

The bright winged sun,
mild moon,
even wisdom and virtue
cannot protect us from you.

Guide us.
Save us from
arousing your anger.
Grace us with peace.

The Furies

Daughters of Hades
and Persephone
you are famous
for giving good advice.

With piercing eyes
of vision unconfined,
knowing all secrets
you see every deed.

With Fate you walk
in darkness
eager to punish
injustice.

Your eyes
of life-destroying light
are strong with revenge,
sharp with torture.

Search us.
Find us clean.
Greet us
when we pass.

Melinoe

Hades seduced
your mother Persephone,
by the mournful
flow of the Styx.

You are half dark,
like your father Hades.
You are half light
like your mother Persephone.

When men sleep
you frighten them
with ghosts
bright as dreams.

Darkly visible
in the night,
suddenly clear
to startled sight

you inspire terror.
Daughter of Kore,
free us from
imaginary fears.

Fortune

Your power is obscure
yet universal.

Some of us praise you
for the gift of wealth.

Others mourn in bitterness
your refusal to bless.

You give deep distress
and triumphant joy.

Gentle Tyche,
grace us with abundance.

Spirit

Soul of the butterfly,
strange angel of fate,
you are the source of life.

You are far traveling Zeus,
terrible, yet gentle,
strongest God.

You give pleasant wealth
or revenge and torture.
You give joy and shelter
or affliction and disease.

You suppress
even necessities.

Your omnipotence is
the key to sorrow and delight.
Sweep away the seeds
of exhausting worry.

We honor you,
grant us glorious days,
ease us into Night.

Ino

Sea Goddess,
you nursed Dionysos,
we honor you.

You are deep
as Ocean,
restless as waves,
bright as Dawn on water.

Guide our ships at sea.
Protect us from ruin.

Palaimon

Your father Athamas
killed your brother
Larchus then chased you
and your mother Ino
off a cliff into the sea.

Remembering Ino
nursed Dionysos
Zeus transformed you
into the dolphin God
and Goddess of the sea.

We honor you,
save us from
raging waves.

The Muses

No desire is stronger
than lust for your light.
We honor you.

Speak, Kalliope.
Beautiful voice,
inspire heroic epic.

Klio, tell us history.
Erato, awaken love.
Euterpe, inspire music.
Melpomene, tell tragedy.
Polyhymnia, teach imitation.
Terpsichore, show us dance.
Thalia, give us comedy.
Ourania, inspire astronomy.

Awaken virtue,
train the mind,
nurse the soul,
show us what is right.

Lend us your light.

Memory

Mother of Muses,
we honor you.

You are free
of forgetfulness.

You give thought
and reason.

Wake truth
sleeping in our hearts.

Excite us to know
the way out of oblivion.

Dawn

You blush red splendor
on the morning horizon.
Your first ray
leads daylight.

You call the sunrise
in the east.
You open the world
of daily work.

Delight of human eyes,
you wake us
from pleasant
but oppressive sleep.

Birds sing.
Animals bark and bray.
Choirs sing.
Everywhere we greet you.

Even the fish in the deep
rejoice in renewed color.
Rose fingered Dawn,
shine forever us.

Themis

Daughter of the sky,
flower of the Earth,
mother of prophecy,
we honor you.

Mother of the four Seasons,
first oracle,
you reign at Delphi.

Grace us
with foresight.
Teach us
holiness.

North Wind

Winter blast,
you tear the deep
surrounding air.

Your power
exposes us
to ice and snow.

Boreas,
we honor you.

Warm your clouds,
empty the skies
of mist and rain.

Grace us
with temperance
and sunshine.

West Wind

Refreshed workers
smile at your sweetness
when you cross the sea
to fill meadows
with gentle sounds.

Son of Dawn,
ships cut smooth
when you fill sails.

Zephyr, husband of Iris,
golden winged
rainy wind of rainbows,
we honor you.

Give wing to seed.
Grace us
with your gentle breath.

South Wind

Your wings whip wet air
into clouds you carry
over the sea,
over the shore,
valleys and hills
to the shoulders
of Olympos
where you release
drenching rain
to refresh the Earth.

We honor you,
give us water.

Ocean

Father of Gods,
animals and men,
we honor you.

Swiftly flowing
waves speak your name
at the limits of Earth.

Father of rivers,
fresh water springs,
and far spreading seas,

Okeanos,
son of ancient Night,
protect us.

Hestia

Daughter of Kronos,
venerable guardian
of the hearth,
we honor you.

You protect
the foundation
of every house
of Gods or men.

Your beauty
and laughter
inspire trust.
Give us health.

Help us discover
the necessity
of hospitality.
Teach us patience.

Sleep

King of the Gods,
animals and men,
we honor you.

Everyone knows you.
You bind us
in invisible chains.

You give rest
from weary work
and gnawing worry.

With pleasing gentleness
you give sweet solace
to every affliction.

Dream

Source of oracles,
we honor you.

In gloom of night
through sleep's sweet silence
creep up softly
to whisper in the mind.

Waking insight,
reunite the silent soul
with Fate.

The wicked never see you
but sense you lurking.
You make them pensive with fear.

You give them no warnings,
no advice, no technique.
They are blind.

Friend to the just,
inspire us
with glimpses of bliss.

Give us hope
and wisdom to know
the language of Fate.

Teach us ways
to avoid suffering.
Show us how
to please the Gods.

Give us tranquility.
Reveal the concealed
signatures of Fate.

Death

King of every tribe,
you choose our time,
we honor you.

With your perpetual sleep
you break the hold
of the soul on the body.

You take every one.
You show no mercy,
not even to babies.

You slay the athlete,
the strong man,
the most vigorous,
no one is safe.

You end every work.
You are judgment
and forgiveness.

No vow can shake your purpose.
No prayer can control you.
Grant us healthy old age
and freedom from forgetfulness.

Notes

1. For a literal translation see Apostolos N. Athanassakis, *The Orphic Hymns: Text, Translation and Notes* (Missoula: Scholars Press, 1977).

2. Joseph Breslin, *A Greek Prayer* (Malibu: J. Paul Getty Museum, n.d.); Larry J. Alderink, *Creation and Salvation in Ancient Orphism* (Chico: Scholar's Press, 1981), 78; W. K. C. Guthrie, *Orpheus and Greek Religion* (London: Methuen, 1952), 171; W. K. C. Guthrie, *The Greeks and their Gods* (Boston: Beacon, 1951), 322; J. E. Harrison, *Prolegomena to the Study of Greek Religion* (Cambridge: Cambridge University Press, 1903), 573. For recent discoveries of gold sheets in Thessaly, Italy and Crete see Albert Henrichs, "Changing Dionysiac Identities," in *Jewish and Christian Self-Definition*, ed. Meyer and Sanders, vol. 3 (Philadelphia: Fortress Press, 1982), 154.

3. Harrison, *Prolegomena*, 597.

4. Chrysippos, the Stoic philosopher from Cilicia east of Syria, 280 B.C., defined them as "writings about divine matters" (Guthrie, *Orpheus and Greek Religion*, 201). For *teletas* see Liddell and Scott, ed., *Greek-English Lexicon* (Oxford: Oxford University Press, 1987). Pausanius, *Description of Greece* translated by Anonymous (Thomas Taylor) (London: 1824), book 3, 245. Also see Alderink, *Creation and Salvation in Ancient Orphism*; Guthrie, *Orpheus and Greek Religion*, 201–203.

5. *The Orphic Poems* might be a better title for the Hymns as we have them.

6. Guthrie, *Orpheus and Greek Religion*, 59; for Aristotle on Orpheus, 12, 58, 244; and Alderink, *Creation and Salvation*, 56–59. Kern argues the name and whole myth of Orpheus was invented by Onomakritos in that century; see Alderink, *Creation and Salvation*, 68; for Onomakritos, 13, 59; for whether Orpheus lived, 4, 9, 11, 53, 56.

7. For a modern discussion of others in Greek history of the name Orpheus see Guthrie, *Orpheus and Greek Religion*, 217. Taylor follows Proklos, Gyraldus, the fathers Vossius and Eschenbach, and others, calling

Onomakritos the fourth Orpheus and author of the Hymns; see "A Dissertation on the Life and Theology of Orpheus," *The Hymns of Orpheus* (Los Angeles: Philosophical Research Society, 1981), 10–13.

8. "They are the words of the poet Ibykos who lived in the sixth century B.C." (Guthrie, *Orpheus and Greek Religion,* 1).

9. Anthony Rooley, *Performance: Revealing the Orpheus Within* (Dorset: Element, 1990), 78.

10. Robert Graves, *The Greek Myths* (New York: Braziller, 1957), 402.

11. From the ancient Greek *orphanos,* orphan.

12. From the ancient Greek *orphnaios,* dark or murky night, darkness.

13. From the ancient Greek *orphinos,* brownish gray mixed from black and a little white and red.

14. Martin Bernal, *Black Athena: the Afro-Asiatic Roots of Classical Civilization* (New Brunswick: Rutgers University Press, 1987), vol. 1, 71; Bernal believes Orpheus is the ancient Greek mutation of the ancient Egyptian Earth god Geb, vol. 2, 245.

15. Guthrie, *Orpheus and Greek Religion,* 61. All translations from Greek are mine unless otherwise noted; I have depended heavily on Guthrie's translations.

16. *Ibid.*

17. *Ibid.*

18. *Ibid.*

19. William Blake Tyrrell, *Amazons: A Study in Athenian Mythmaking* (London: John Hopkins, 1984).

20. Pausanias, *Description of Greece* 8.30.3–4.

21. Probably Mount Pangaios in Macedonia, where the Muses gathered the

pieces of Orpheus. Others give Mount Haimos among the Odrysai in Thrace where the stone tablets of Orpheus were kept, Mount Serrhion in Cicconian Thrace, and Mount Pieria on the border of Thrace and Macedonia. See Guthrie, *Orpheus and Greek Religion*, 13, 32; Macchioro, *From Orpheus to Paul: A History of Orphism*, 142.

22. See Lee Irwin, "The Orphic Mystery: Harmony and Mediation," in *Alexandria 1*, edited by David Fideler, 37–55 (Grand Rapids: Phanes Press, 1991). For death of Orpheus see Alderink, *Creation and Salvation*, 10.

23. *Dr. Smith's Classical Dictionary* (London: John Murray, 1894), 485; Lee Irwin, "The Orphic Mystery," 47; Harrison, *Prolegomena*, 466. "Others have said his wife died before him, and that for her sake he came to Aornon in Thesprotis where there was an Oracle of the Dead. They say he thought the soul of Eurydice followed him, but turning he lost her and committed suicide. Thracians say the nightengales who nest on his tomb sing more loudly and sweetly" (Pausanius, *Description of Greece* 8.30.4–5). Plato said, "Orpheus was not brave enough to die for love so the Gods gave him not Eurydice, but a shadow. Musicians usually lack courage" (Alderink, *Creation and Salvation*, 10).

24. Guthrie, *Orpheus and Greek Religion*, 15.

25. Guthrie, *The Greeks and their Gods*, 89, 315.

26. Harrison, *Prolegomena*, 459, 545, 573; also Alderink, *Creation and Salvation*, 100, note 8; Guthrie, *Orpheus and Greek Religion*, 110ff.

27. "Only two places can put in a strong claim to have been its original home . . . Athens, the home of Onamokritos, which claimed to have had the Mysteries of Orpheus revealed to her, and South Italy, the home of Pythagoreanism and of writers of Orphic poems" (Guthrie, *The Greeks and their Gods*, 314).

28. Guthrie quotes Professor Cornford's *From Religion to Philosophy*. "Whether or not we accept the hypothesis of direct influence from Persia on the Ionian Greeks in the sixth century, any student of Orphic and Pythagorean thought cannot fail to see that the similarities between it and Persian religion are so close as to warrant our regarding them as expressions of the same view of life. . . ." Guthrie, *Orpheus and Greek Religion*,

87, 91, 143; Guthrie discusses Gruppe's belief that "periodical renewal of the universe myths as in the Orphic Mysteries started in Babylonia and spread to the Near East, especially Syria and Asia Minor." Gruppe points to Asia Minor as the home of the Phanes myth, 98.

29. For *-eus* see Guthrie, *Orpheus and Greek Religion*, 68, note 27. For Orpheus as a "prehistoric Thracian," see Guthrie, *The Greeks and their Gods*, 314. "All this converges towards the conclusion that behind the traditional Orpheus stood a primitive shaman who first introduced into Greece an ecstatic religion consisting mainly in visions of the afterlife . . . like Earthly life but flushed with sunshine" (Macchioro, *From Orpheus to Paul*, 134); for the resemblance of Orphism to the Native American Ghost Dance, 131; but doubting Macchioro's position see Guthrie, *Orpheus and Greek Religion*, 68, note 24, and Alderink, *Creation and Salvation*, 7, 9. ". . . although Orpheus may be very ancient, Orphism was established in the Sixth Century in close connection with Pythagoreanism" (Martin Bernal, *Black Athena*, vol. 1, 71).

30. For Agriope see Guthrie, *Orpheus and Greek Religion*, 29–30; Harrison, *Prolegomena*, 603; Macchioro, *From Orpheus to Paul*, 136. Professor Rose in *Handbook of Greek Mythology* argued that the Eurydice myth was very ancient but few agree.

31. Harrison, *Prolegomena*, 604.

32. *Ibid.*, 604. See also Macchioro, *From Orpheus to Paul*, 136.

33. Guthrie, *Orpheus and Greek Religion*, 216, 234.

34. Olympiodorus, the teacher of Proklos, said Plato "is full of echoes of Orpheus" (Guthrie, *The Greeks and their Gods*, 312). "The later Neoplatonists made a point of illustrating a sentence of Plato, whenever they could, by a quotation from Orphic poems" (Guthrie, *Orpheus and Greek Religion*, 72; see also 157, 238, 242). Harrison writes: "Plato so detested the lower side of Orphic rites that perhaps he only half realized the extent of his debts" (Harrison, *Prolegomena*, 578, 648).

35. Virgil, *Aeneid* 6; Guthrie, *The Greeks and their Gods*, 324; Harrison, *Prolegomena*, 583.

36. Harrison, *Prolegomena*, 473.

37. Kathleen Raine, *Blake and Tradition* (Princeton: Bollingen, 1962).

38. Guthrie, *Orpheus and Greek Religion*, 217.

39. The Lykomidai family of Athens were said to be the hereditary singers of the Orphic Hymns; Guthrie, *Orpheus and Greek Religion*, 126. At the beginning of the third century A.D., the Athenian Philostratos wrote that the prophet Apollonios of Tyana was shocked by the behavior of the Athenians at the rites of Dionysos. "It shocked him to see them 'dancing lascivious dances to the flute, and in the midst of the poetry and hymns of Orpheus play acting now as the Hours, now as Nymphs and now as Bacchants'" (Guthrie, *Orpheus and Greek Religion*, 259).

40. *Ibid.*, 136; also see McGinty, *Dionysos and Interpretation*, 193.

41. Guthrie, *Orpheus and Greek Religion*, 26ff; also see McGinty, *Dionysos and Interpretation*, 62, 193, and 225, note 25.

42. Guthrie, *Orpheus and Greek Religion*, 61.

43. *Ibid.*, 16. If a carved wooden phallus was the object in the *likna*, the missing limb or heart of Dionysos taken away by Athene in a basket, it would seem to be the Greek version of the missing phallus of Osiris in the Mysteries of Isis. C. Kerenyi, *The Gods of the Greeks* (London: Thames and Hudson, 1979), 255–56.

44. "I have no difficulty accepting the possibility that the Eleusinian cult of Archaic Greece was the descendent of an Egyptian foundation made there seven hundred years earlier" (Bernal, *Black Athena*, vol. 1, 69). Thomas Taylor writes: "The Orphic Hymns which exist at present were the very hymns which were used in the Eleusinian Mysteries" in his Pausanius, *Description of Greece*, book 3, 245. Also see Guthrie, *Orpheus and Greek Religion*, 135, 211; Harrison, *Prolegomena*, 548; Thomas Taylor, *The Eleusinian and Bacchic Mysteries* (San Diego: Wizards Bookshelf, 1980).

45. Alderink, *Creation and Salvation*, 89.

46. Harrison, *Prolegomena*, 135, 514.

47. *Ibid.*, 476.

48. Pythagoras taught veiled by a *synode* like Hebrew, Islamic or Native American prophets praying under their robes or blankets. Macchioro, *From Orpheus to Paul*, 119.

49. Kallimachos was a grammarian and poet. The chief librarian of the Library of Alexandria (250 B.C.), he compiled its catalog. Apollonius Rhodius was his student.

50. Harrison, *Prolegomena*, 403, 520, 534. "In a carnival mummery or ritual play of modern Thrace (1935), Babo (a word in general local use meaning an old woman) is the name of the old woman who carries about a child in a basket shaped cradle called a *liknon*" (Guthrie, *Orpheus and Greek Religion*, 137). For *liknon* as fruit basket see McGinty, *Dionysos and Interpretation*, 217; for *liknon* and *Dionysos Liknites*, 118, 120. Graves says the *liknon* was made of woven willow; Robert Graves, *The White Goddess* (New York: Farrar, 1948), 144.

51. "Orpheus, whatever may have been his origin, appears in history as a human prophet and teacher whose doctrine was embedded in a collection of writings" (Guthrie, *Orpheus and Greek Religion*, 9). "The trouble is that Orphism always was a literature, first and foremost" (*Ibid.*, 10).

52. Ion of Chios, the friend of Aeschylus and playwright rival to Euripides in fifth century B.C. Athens, wrote that Pythagoras composed writings under the name Orpheus. Cicero called Aeschylus a Pythagorean; the lost play of Aeschylus, *The Bassarids*, was about the death of Orpheus; see Guthrie, *Orpheus and Greek Religion*, 216, 234; also see McGinty, *Dionysos and Interpretation*, 217; Graves, *White Goddess*, 236–7; and S. K. Heniger, *Touches of Sweet Harmony* (San Marino: Huntington Library, 1974).

53. Otto Kern, *Orphicorum Fragmenta*. (Berlin: Weidmann, 1922), frag. 234.

54. "The *Orpheotelestai* of Plato are exclusively men" (Marcel Detienne, *Dionysos Slain* [Baltimore: Johns Hopkins, 1977], 68). Arthur Evans

disagrees; see Evans, *The God of Ecstasy*, 159. Guthrie thinks this may have been the case in late Orphism but not in early; Guthrie, *Orpheus and Greek Religion*, 50, 202.

55. Plato, *Republic* 364B.

56. Kern argued the hymns were collected and used at the city of Pergamon, in a famously fertile and beautiful valley in Asia Minor, in the temple of Demeter; see Guthrie, *Orpheus and Greek Religion*, 15, 136, 256, 258, 260.

57. "Onomakritos was one of the committee appointed by Peisistratos to edit the text of Homer and among his colleagues were Orpheus of Kroton and Zopyros of Herakleia" (Guthrie, *Orpheus and Greek Religion*, 217). Guthrie follows this tradition back through Proklos to Asklepiades of Myrlea, a grammarian of the second century B.C. Kroton was the city of Pythagoras' school in Southern Italy. Some have argued Pythagoras invented Orpheus. For Onomakritos, see Guthrie, *Orpheus*, 5, 14, 107, 115; Guthrie reminds us Onomakritos was not the only mutator of the Hymns, 15.

58. McGinty, *Dionysos and Interpretation*, 111, note 29.

59. Guthrie, *Orpheus and Greek Religion*, 13.

60. Kern argues the name and whole myth of Orpheus was invented by Onomakritos in that century; see Guthrie, *Orpheus and Greek Religion*, 68; also see Guthrie, *The Greeks and their Gods*, 331.

61. Joseph Fontenrose believes the myth is pre-Orphic; see Joseph Fontenrose, *Python* (Berkeley: University of California Press, 1959), 123. Guthrie disagrees: "The myth of the child Dionysos and his playthings was first expounded at Athens in the sixth century" (Guthrie, *Orpheus and Greek Religion*, 126).

62. Guthrie quotes Plato: "When the Creator first made the individual souls, he made them 'equal in number to the stars,' and assigned each one to a star,' and while they were still on the stars he taught them the nature of the Universe, and what was to be their own fate, namely to be implanted in bodies. . . When they had been implanted in bodies by the workings of necessity . . . first of all the faculty of sensation, one and the same for all,

would be naturally aroused in them as a result of violent impressions, and secondly love, mingled with pleasure and pain, and in addition to these fear and anger and all the passions which either result from these or are their contraries. If they conquered these passions, they would live in righteousness, but if they were conquered by them, with unrighteousness; and the one who lived his appointed time well, would travel again to dwell in his proper star, and live a blessed life according to his true nature.'" (Guthrie, *Orpheus and Greek Religion*, 186).

63. Plato comments: "It seems to me the followers of Orpheus just say *soma* [the body] since they say the soul is punished for whatever evil it did by restriction to a body" (*Kratylos*, 400c); also "I once heard one of our sages say that we are now dead, and the body is our tomb" (*Gorgias* 493A, translated by Lamb from Alderink, *Creation and Salvation in Ancient Orphism*). Guthrie quotes Plato's *Phaedrus*: "mortals are immortal souls trapped in body; immortals are souls free of body" (Guthrie, *Orpheus and Greek Religion*, 167). Aristotle in *Proteptikos* frag. 60 compares the angst of soul in body with the torture practiced by Etruskan pirates: tying a victim face to face with a corpse; Guthrie, *Orpheus and Greek Religion*, 156. Also see Harrison, *Prolegomena*, 604. Dodds says *soma sema* is not Orphic; E. R. Dodds, *The Greeks and the Irrational* (Cambridge: Cambridge University Press, 1964), 170. Also see Alderink, *Creation and Salvation in Ancient Orphism*, 60, 99; McGinty, *Dionysos and Interpretation*, 107.

64. Lethe: oblivion, seclusion, hiddenness; see Guthrie, *Orpheus and Greek Religion*, 66, 109.

65. Guthrie, *The Greeks and their Gods*, 320. Also see Alderink, *Creation and Salvation in Ancient Orphism*.

66. Georg Feuerstein, *Yoga: The Technology of Ecstasy* (Los Angeles: Tarcher, 1989), 129.

67. For an argument that Titans are the mythic relic of a historical war, see McGinty, *Dionysos and Interpretation*, 109. For an argument that the Titan myth is Neoplatonic but not Orphic see Alderink, *Creation and Salvation*, 66. To Neoplatonists Dionysos is the soul. The soul is fascinated by its distorted reflection and by the spinning tops (planets) of the Titans (the elemental forces of the physical universe). These forces of

incarnation tear the soul into seven pieces; that is, the soul divides into the limbs and organs of the body. The Orphics believed the organs formed each other "like plaiting a net." Dionysos is God of Liberation: the soul realizing itself immortal; Guthrie, *Orpheus and Greek Religion*, 14ff, 72, 75, 101, 156; Alderink, *Creation and Salvation*, 66, 109 ; and Thomas Taylor, *The Eleusinian and Bacchic Mysteries*.

68. Guthrie, *Orpheus and Greek Religion*, 23.

69. *Ibid.*, 13.

70. *Ibid.*, 93.

71. Eisler believed Orphics showed Orpheus crucified; see Guthrie, *Orpheus and Greek Religion*, 261, 266, 338ff. For an example of Orphic crucifixion, see the 3rd c. A.D. cylinder seal or amulet of a man crucified on a cross like an anchor with the words *Orpheos Bakkikos* to the side and a moon and seven stars overhead, Guthrie, *Orpheus and Greek Religion*, 265; Guthrie believes the issue is not influence of Orphism on Chrisianity but common elements in mystery religions, 23ff, 133, 160, 207, 261, 267. Arthur Evans reminds us: "The Orphic concept of the Titanic taint in human nature was magnified into the doctrine of original sin"; see Arthur Evans, *The God of Ecstasy*, 170. Also see Macchioro, *From Orpheus to Paul*. Guthrie discusses Boulanger's argument that the name Orpheus was adopted by South Italian writers of the third century because Orpheus was widely believed to have been earlier than Homer and therefore a traditional authority to quote against Bible-quoting Christians; see Guthrie, *Orpheus and Greek Religion*, 14. The later Neoplatonists "made a point of illustrating a sentence of Plato, whenever they could, by a quotation from Orphic poems. . . . The later Neoplatonists found themselves among the last defenders of pagan Hellenic culture against the rapidly advancing power of Christianity. . . . The best hope now lay . . . in saying 'What you believe does represent a profound and valuable truth, but it is a truth that has been known to us Greeks since the dawn of our history'" (Guthrie, *Orpheus and Greek Religion*, 72).

72. For the Orphic wheel see Guthrie, *Orpheus and Greek Religion*, 142, 208. Also see Harrison, *Prolegomena*, 590. Alderink doubts the escape from the weary wheel is Orphic; Alderink, *Creation and Salvation*, 3, 9.

73. Guthrie, *Orpheus and Greek Religion*, 14. For Orphic depravity see J. H. Croon, "De Orphiek," *Forum der Letteren* 6:17 (1965).

74. Guthrie, *Orpheus and Greek Religion*, 109, 111; also see McGinty, *Dionysos and Interpretation*, 55.

75. Jane Harrison believes the "almost ceremonial tenderness shown to animals by the Pythagorean Orphics is an Egyptian rather than Greek characteristic." McGinty, *Dionysos and Interpretation*, 590. In *Dionysos Slain*, Marcel Detienne argues the myth of Dionysos and the Titans was no more or less than an Orphic condemnation of animal sacrifice.

76. Alderink, *Creation and Salvation*, 73–78.

77. Plato refers to those who don't eat meat as following the "Orphic Life"; see Plato, *Laws* 782C; also see Alderink, *Creation and Salvation*, 80. Marcel Detienne writes of the Orphics: "the consumption of meat effects a distance between gods and men in the very movement that accomplishes communication between this earthly world and that of the divine powers. Hence forth the acts of each sacrificer will serve as a reminder that by eating flesh destined for corruption, men are condemned to hunger and death, while the gods enjoy the privilege of perfumed smoke . . . the incorruptible substances that the flames of the sacrificial fire have transformed" (Marcel Detienne, "Culinary Practices and the Practice of Sacrifice," in *The Cuisine of Sacrifice* [Chicago: University of Chicago Press, 1989]).

78. *Republic* 364B.

79. Harrison, *Prolegomena*, 645.

80. Joseph Campbell, *The Masks of God: Occidental Mythology* (New York: Viking, 1964), 183.

81. *Ibid.*, 184.

82. The Orphic Hymns suggest appropriate incense under their titles: storax, poppy, myrrh and frankincense, alone or in combinations; Guthrie, *Orpheus and Greek Religion*, 256. Apostolos Athanassikis and Thomas Taylor give the appropriate incense with each hymn in their translations.

The *lyra-da-braccio* was an instrument much loved by Renaissance humanists. It was a bowed instrument, but tuned to play chords, and produced a resonant sound something like a harmonium.

83. Anthony Rooley, *Performance: Revealing the Orpheus Within* (Shaftesbury: Element, 1990), 7, 74, 85; Bernal, *Black Athena*, vol. 1, 155ff; Thomas Moore, *The Planets Within* (Lewisburg: Bucknell University Press, 1982); Eisenbeichler, editor, *Ficino and Renaissance Neoplatonism* (Ottawa: University of Toronto, 1986); D. P. Walker, *Spiritual and Demonic Magic from Ficino to Campanella* (London: Watkins, 1975); John Warden, editor, *Orpheus: the Metamorphoses of a Myth* (Toronto: University of Toronto Press, 1982), 85; Henry Purcell, *Orpheus Britannicus* (London, 1698). Also see the 14th century "Lay of Sir Orfeo," Anonymous, *The Lay of Sir Orfeo*, translated by J. R. R. Tolkien (Boston: Houghton Mifflin, 1988).

84. "Voltaire, for one, insisted on interpreting the Orphic mystery religion as an advanced monotheistic cult which had surrounded itself with secrecy from fear of violence at the hands of a gross populace. Diderot, capable of giving a discriminating account of Orpheus' life and death, his cult and influence, could resist the lure of rationalism no better. After citing some ancient authors on Orpheus' magic powers, he quoted a more congenial passage from Horace's *Ars poetica* which implied that Orpheus was an adroit imposter who had claimed divine sanction for reasonable codes of conduct in order to prevent his savage followers from tearing each other to pieces" (Peter Gay, *The Enlightenment: An Interpretation* [New York: Knopf, 1967], 83). For Elizabethan Orphism see S. K. Heniger, *Touches of Sweet Harmony.*

85. Harrison, *Prolegomena*, 421.

86. Like the Tantric Sri Yantra diagram showing the Great Goddess geometrically divided into Gods and Goddesses. For gods as aspects of God and Orphic syncretism see Guthrie, *Orpheus and Greek Religion*, 100, 251. Taylor's discussion of Orphic theology, "A Dissertation on the Life and Theology of Orpheus" in *The Hymns of Orpheus*, based largely on Gyraldus and the Neoplatonists, resembles Blake's Zoa and the Tantric Shiva-Shakti: the gods and goddesses are joined in active and passive pairs. Blake read Taylor's translation of the Hymns. See David Erdman, *Blake: Prophet Against Empire* (New York: Anchor, 1969), 177; see especially

Kathleen Raine, *Blake and Antiquity*, and George Harper, *Neoplatonism of William Blake* (Chapel Hill: University of North Carolina Press, 1961). For a modern discussion of Orphic theology see Alderink, *Creation and Salvation*, 25.

87. For monotheism see Guthrie, *Orpheus and Greek Religion*, 100, 145 note 27. Also Harrison, *Prolegomena*, 32, 626.

Annotated Bibliography

Alderink, Larry J. *Creation and Salvation in Ancient Orphism.* Chico: Scholar's Press, 1981. Indispensable comprehensive study of the central Orphic myths. Detailed criticism of earlier studies. Translation and discussion of the important Derveni papyrus, discovered in 1962 in Northern Greece, one of the earliest Orphic artifacts (4th c. B.C.), not fully published yet (1981). "It was found in one of four graves with a buried warrior's equipment, a spear and a javelin; a nearby tomb contained a krater portraying Dionysos surrounded by naked satyrs and maenads, wooing Ariadne," 26. This book is an education in critical scholarship, method and objectivity. Includes pithy translations of Burkert; valuable quotes from H. J. Rose, like this about the evidence for organized Orphic religion: "In somewhat the same manner there has never been a church called Puritan . . . yet 'Puritan' and 'Puritanism' meant something in the religious history of Great Britain and the U.S.A.", 15. Lucid analysis of Pindar. Hermeneutics, Wittgenstein and Venn diagrams expertly used to clarify:

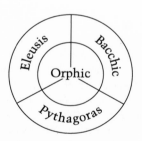

Alderink mentions a Jewish Orphism between 2nd c. B.C. and 2nd c. A.D., 18. He argues that the Orphics did not believe in transmigration, but did believe souls pre-exist and survive bodies, 58. But Arthur Evans points out: "The notion of Larry Alderink that Orphism is merely 'a mood or a spirit which animates selected literary texts' (Alderink, 19) is refuted by Plato, who explicitly says in *The Republic* (364E) that the Orphics used their books in ritual practices" (Arthur Evans, *The God of Ecstasy*, 158).

Atchity, Kenneth with R. C. Hogart and Doug Price, eds. *Critical Essays on Homer.* Boston: G.K. Hall, 1987. See especially Norman Austin's "Archery at the Dark of the Moon" and Paolo Vivante's "Rose Fingered Dawn and the Idea of Time."

Athanassakis, Apostolos, trans. *The Orphic Hymns.* Missoula: Society of Biblical Literature, 1977. The Greek text with an eloquent literal translation.

Bachofen, J. J. *Myth, Religion, and Mother Right.* Princeton: Princeton University Press, 1967. Valuable discussions of Dionysos, Aphrodite, Demeter, and Apollo, with emphasis on the suppression of matriarchy. Bachofen, writing in 1861, introduced the word "matriarchy."

Bernabe, Albertus. *Orphai Concordantia.* New York: Weidmann, 1988. Indispensable concordance to the Greek text.

Bernal, Martin. *Black Athene: the Afro-Asiatic Roots of Classical Civilization.* New Brunswick: Rutgers University Press, 1987. Monumental study of the "fabrication of Greece" by European scholars from the eighteenth to the twentieth century. The first two volumes of the projected four volumes are available (1992). The third volume will contain a section on Orpheus and Orphism. Bernal argues against the Aryan bias that sees classical Greek civilization as an evolution of the culture of the Indo-Aryan invaders. Bernal reminds us that ancient Greek sources give Egypt and Phoenicia as the roots of Classical Civilization. In the prehistoric period of Greek history, Egypt at the height of its power may have colonized Greece; Athens, the city of Athene may have begun as an Egyptian colony named after the Egyptian Goddess Neith. The Phoenicians had a colony on the Greek island Thera.

Borgeard, Philippe. *The Cult of Pan in Ancient Greece.* Translated by Atlass and Redfield. Chicago: University of Chicago Press, 1988. Study of Pan cult with detailed attention to festivals and Pan's associations with the Nymphs, Artemis, the Satyrs, and Hekate. Discussion of Nympholepsy, a condition suffered by ancient Greeks from Athenian teenagers to mighty Socrates himself, whereby a person in the woods would suddenly be overcome by intense elation. This was considered possession by a nymph. Some would run away into the woods and never return.

Breslin, Joseph. *A Greek Prayer.* Malibu: J. Paul Getty Museum, n.d. Museum pamphlet.

Campbell, Joseph. *The Masks of God: Occidental Mythology.* New York: Viking, 1964. A few important words about the origins of Orphism and its similarities to Hindu Shiva worship.

———. *The Mythic Image.* Princeton: Princeton University Press, 1974. The world as dream and other themes of Yoga traced through worldwide mutations and parallels from the Australian Bushmen to the ancient civilizations of Greece, China and Africa. Beautifully illustrated.

Cook, Arthur Bernard. *Zeus: A Study in Ancient Religion.* 3 vols. Cambridge: Cambridge University Press, 1914–1940. The classic study of the Zeus cult. Three volumes of lucid and exhaustive scholarship. The index is an education in the attributes and myths of the Greek Gods and Goddesses.

Danielou, Alain. *Shiva and Dionysus.* New York: Inner Traditions, 1984. Startling apocalyptic mysticism and revelations of similarities in Greek and Hindu religion by a devoted student of both. Danielou, author of the classic *Hindu Polytheism* (Princeton: Princeton University Press, 1964), was a great musician, artist and athlete, and one of the first Anglo Saxons enrolled as a Hindu in the central shrine of Hinduism.

Detienne, Marcel. "Culinary Practices and the Spirit of Sacrifice." In *The Cuisine of Sacrifice,* edited by Detienne and Vernant. Chicago: University of Chicago Press, 1989. Witty, sane essay reminding us most ancient Greek participants in sacrifice ate the animals they slaughtered; the Gods and Goddesses feasted on smoke because immortals couldn't hunger for corruptible and therefore corrupted food.

———. *Dionysos Slain.* Translated by Muellner and Muellner. Baltimore: John Hopkins University Press, 1977. Penetrating discussion of the Dionysian myth of sacrifice with a large chapter on Orphism and Orphic prohibitions against animal sacrifice and meat eating. Albert Henrichs argues that Detienne confuses myth and cult; see Albert Henrichs *"in* of Self, Suffering, and Violence: The Modern View of Dio⸳

Nietzsche to Girard," *Harvard Studies in Classical Philology*, 88 (1984), 205–240. For criticism of Henrichs' position see Arthur Evans, *The God of Ecstasy*, 156.

Dodds, E. R. *The Greeks and the Irrational*. Cambridge: Cambridge University Press, 1964. Dodds discusses the differences between Orpheus and Orphism, reminding us that even primary Orphic materials such as the gold plates, Aristophanes' *The Birds*, and the myths of Plato may not be Orphic. He finds no evidence to believe that *soma sema* is Orphic. Dodds proposes Scythian or Thracian shamanism as the origin of Orphic myth. Careful of Linforth's analytical rigor, Dodds concludes Orpheus was a "mythical shaman or prototype of shamans." For a summary of Dodds see Alderink, *Creation and Salvation*, 14; and McGinty, *Dionysos and Interpretation*, 181.

Encyclopaedia Britannica, 1948 edition, s.v., "Aphrodite," "Apollo," "Ares," "Artemis," "Athena," "Dionysus," "Greek Religion," "Hecate," "Hephaestus," "Hera," "Hercules," "Hermes," "Orpheus," "Poseidon," "Thyrsus," "Zeus." Informative summaries attentive to details of cult.

Evans, Arthur. *The God of Ecstasy*. New York: St. Martin's Press, 1988. Study of Dionysos focusing on *The Bacchae* of Euripides. Includes an excellent translation of *The Bacchae*, and a wealth of useful quotations from the *Dionysica* of Nonnos, and from Plutarch, for example: "Plutarch mentions that Philip and Olympias, the parents of Alexander the Conqueror, first met when they were both initiated into an Orphic cult in Samothrace in the North," 157. Evans surveys the myth of Dionysos from its origins to its modern variations. Along the way he analyzes Athenian law, ancient Greek attitudes toward homosexuality, and the plight of women in ancient Greece: in "democratic" Athens rape was usually considered the victim's fault, the law compelled husbands to divorce raped wives, and punishment for rape was "only a fine," 16. Lucid chapters on Rome and India (including an essential criticism of Alain Danielou's work) and a chapter on Dionysos and Christ with comments on the Witch Persecution. Evans summarizes and critiques Albert Henrichs's important articles on Dionysos and Orphism.

╌╍ell, Lewis R. *The Cults of the Greek States*. Oxford: Oxford University
ᵗᶦᵛᵉ ╌ ╌ The classic collection on Ancient Greek religion. Exhaus-
╌╌ ⌐d

Fideler, David. "Orpheus and the Mysteries of Harmony," *Gnosis* 27 (Spring 1993). Explores the magical power of music, the story of Orpheus, and the nature of musical harmony in ancient cosmological symbolism, both pagan and Christian.

Fontenrose, Joseph. *The Delphic Oracle.* Berkeley: University of California Press, 1978. Bits and pieces about Orpheus in the notes on this collection of questions and answers of the Oracle.

———. *Python.* Berkeley: University of California Press, 1959. Interesting parallels to Orpheus in the classic study on the mythology of the Oracle at Delphi.

Garland, Robert. *The Greek Way of Death.* Ithaca: Cornell University Press, 1985. Meticulous survey of ancient Greek funeral customs, mythology and folklore.

Graves, Robert. *The White Goddess.* London: Faber and Faber, 1948. Graves' controversial study of tree alphabets and the origins of the muse myth occasionally sheds an interesting light on Orphism. "A famous Greek picture by Polygnotus at Delphi represented Orpheus as receiving the gift of mystic eloquence by touching willow trees in the Grove of Persephone," 144. According to Graves in the theology brought by Orphics to Rome, Hera is "physical nature," Zeus is the "impregnating or animating principle" symbolized by the sun, and Athene is the "directing wisdom behind the universe," symbolized by the moon, 382, perhaps because observing the moon's phases and tides taught humans to measure.

———. *The Greek Myths.* New York: Braziller, 1957. Wonderful handbook collection of complete Greek Myths supported by exotic White Goddess footnotes.

Guthrie, W. K. C. *The Greeks and their Gods.* Boston: Beacon Press, 1951. A brief but informative chapter on Orphism. Among other interesting points, Guthrie reminds us that Empedokles, the "philosopher, scientist, poet, orator, statesman, mystagogue, miracle worker, healer, and claimant to divine honors," as the Oxford Classical Dictionary puts it, was a passionate believer in Orphism. For a summary and criticism of Guthrie see McGinty, *Dionysos and Salvation*, 188.

————. *Orpheus and Greek Religion.* London: Methuen, 1952. The bedrock study of Orphism. A wealth of essential translations including numerous quotes from Proklos. Clear and complete translation and discussion of Plato on Orpheus and reincarnation, 167. "To us the differences between the worship of Olympian Zeus and the mysteries of Demeter may seem as great as those between any two religions of modern times. Yet not only did they never lead to wars or persecutions, but it was perfectly possible for the same man to be a devout participant in both," 7. Excellent bibliography. For a summary of Guthrie see Alderink, *Creation and Salvation,* 11–12; and McGinty, *Dionysos and Interpretation,* 187. Unfortunately, McGinty does not discuss *Orpheus and Greek Religion* in depth.

Harrison, Jane. *Epilogomena to the Study of Greek Religion.* Cambridge: Cambridge University Press, 1921. This short work reflects the influence of Freudianism. As McGinty shows in *Dionysos and Interpretation,* Harrison suffered from a then prevalent belief in the stupidity of primitive man.

————. *Prolegomena to the Study of Greek Religion.* Cambridge: Cambridge University Press, 1903. "Dated," according to McGinty, *Dionysos and Interpretation,* 75; "tendentious pronouncements, programmatic generalizations, heartfelt exhortations, and autobiographical claims and confessions dot her work," McGinty, *Dionysos and Interpretation,* 73. Harrison believed the Dionysian rites were "the product of mental backwardness," McGinty, *Dionysos and Interpretation,* 71ff, 21, 69, 105, 221. Harrison was heavily influenced by the technique and perspective of Frazier's *The Golden Bough.* She argues that the Orphic rites preserved the tribal memory of the original shaman dances. The Maenads, Satyrs, and Koretes were mythic distortions of warriors dancing around the bonfire. Harrison argues the Orphic Mysteries originated in Crete.

————. *Themis: A Study of the Social Origins of Greek Religion.* Cambridge: Cambridge University Press, 1912. Harrison examines how local cult ancestor spirits evolved into Olympian gods. She analyzes a Hymn to the Kouretes for evidence the Titans were initiators at primitive rites. Nilsson dismissed this as "telescoping the millenia," McGinty, *Dionysos and Interpretation,* 223, note 31. The latter half of the book is a discussion of Dike and Themis, Moral Right, and Natural Law heavily influenced by the "sociological evolutionism of Emile Durkheim and

Bergson," McGinty, *Dionysos and Interpretation*, 85, 86. Harrison is "lively, learned, yet unpedantic—and utterly uncontrolled by anything resembling careful logic," as G. S. Kirk wrote, McGinty, *Dionysos and Interpretation*, 211.

Heniger, S. K. *Touches of Sweet Harmony*. San Marino: Huntington Library, 1974. A beautifully written, illustrated and bound study of the influence of Orphism and Pythagoreanism on Shakespeare, Spenser, and the Elizabethans.

Henrichs, Albert. "Response." In *Orphism and Bacchic Mysteries: New Evidence and Old Problems of Interpretation*. Berkeley: The Center for Hermeneutical Studies, Protocol of 28th Colloquy, 1977. Henrichs follows Linforth, doubting the evidence for organized Orphism, 210–211. Evans uses skillful philology to critique Henrichs; see Arthur Evans, *The God of Ecstasy* (New York: St. Martin's Press, 1988), 156.

Irwin, Lee. "The Orphic Mystery: Harmony and Mediation." In *Alexandria 1*, edited by David Fideler, 37–55. Grand Rapids: Phanes, 1991. A concise and comprehensive summary and analysis in a journal with other excellent articles on ancient Greek music and religion.

Jaeger, Werner. *Paideia: the Ideals of Greek Culture*. New York: Oxford University Press, 1948. Several interesting comments on Orphism in this careful three volume study of ancient Greek ideas about education.

Kerenyi, C. *Asklepios*. Princeton: Princeton University Press, 1959. Comprehensive study of the God of Healing. Kerenyi believes the Asklepios cult developed from shamanism. The ancient Greek depiction of Chiron the Centaur reproduced in this book will remind tarot scholars of the Fool card, complete with robe of stars, dog nipping at feet, and pole over shoulder.

———. *Eleusis*. Princeton: Princeton University Press, 1967. Archeological focus in a classic study of the Eleusinian Mysteries. Many references to Orpheus and the Orphic Hymns.

———. *The Gods of the Greeks*. London: Thames and Hudson, 1979. Superior survey of Greek mythology; a scholarly handbook with constant attention to the details of epithets and cult.

————. *Apollo*. Dallas: Spring, 1983. Detailed short study of Apollo revealing the importance of the wolf cult often forgotten or glossed over by Apollonians.

Kern, Otto. *Eine Religionsgeschichtliche Untersuchung*. Berlin: 1920. A brief but concentrated overview of the Orphic cult. Kern reports rumors that Orpheus was the grandfather or otherwise direct ancestor of Homer. Inspiring frontispiece photo of stern, crew cut, long bearded, pioneer Orphic scholar from Bavaria.

————. *Orphicorum Fragmenta*. Berlin: Weidmann, 1922. Meticulous and essential collection of texts.

Liddell and Scott. *Greek-English Lexicon*. Oxford: Oxford University Press, 1987. Indispensable and holy to scholars of ancient Greece.

Linforth, I. M. *The Arts of Orpheus*. Berkeley: University of California Press, 1941. Focus on Orphic influence on Plato and the mainstream Attic culture. Devastating criticism of evidence for Orphism. Linforth argues Orphism never was a common creed and ceremony, it was "a category for those ancients interested in a vast miscellany of myth and religious lore." For a summary of Linforth see Alderink, *Creation and Salvation*, 10–11.

Macchioro, Vittorio D. *From Orpheus to Paul: A History of Orphism*. New York: Henry Holt, 1930. "The summary consists partly of dogmatic assertions, partly of obvious misinterpretations of Aristotle and Plutarch," writes Guthrie, *Orpheus and Greek Religion*, 246; but Macchioro presents a wealth of materials from which to draw one's own interpretation.

McGinty, Park. *Interpretation and Dionysos: Method in the Study of a God*. The Hague: Mouton, 1978. An example of critical excellence, revealing the contexts and biases of the scholars constructing Orphic history. A wealth of quotations, such as Nietszche on the intoxicating effect of Dionysos: "Now all the rigid, hostile barriers which need, caprice or 'insolent fashion' have fixed between men are smashed. Now, with the gospel of the world harmony, everyone feels not only united, reconciled, merged with his neighbor, but one with him, as though the veil of Maya had been torn and only fluttered in tatters before the mysterious primordial One," 40. Essential discussion of Walter F. Otto's important works on Dionysos. Excellent bibliography.

Mead, G. R. S. *Orpheus*. London: Watkins, 1965. Good scholarship from the author of *Thrice-Greatest Hermes*. Fold out chart. A useful overview.

Meyer, Marvin W., ed. *The Ancient Mysteries: A Sourcebook*. San Francisco: Harper and Row, 1987. Modern translations and helpful notes, useful for studies of similarities and differences between the cults of the Euphrates and the Mediterranean.

Moore, Thomas. *The Planets Within*. Bucknell University Press: Lewisburg, 1982. Reprint. Great Barrington: Lindisfarne Press, 1990. Detailed, seminal study of Ficino's fusion of Christian and Classical theology and astrology and its influence on the Italian Renaissance. Foreword by Noel Cobb.

Moulinier, Louis. *Orphee et L'Orphisme a l'Epoque Classique*. Paris, 1955. Brief, but incisive. Moulinier follows Linforth, doubting the evidence. He summarizes the history of argument that the slaughter of Dionysos by the Titans was not necessarily linked to Titanic origin of humanity.

Nilsson, M. P. "Early Orphism and Kindred Religious Movements," *Harvard Theological Review* 28 (1935), 181–230. Nilsson argued from the *liknon* that Dionysos is the "spirit of the fruit of the fields," but later changed his mind, believing the evidence does not connect Dionysos to agriculture. McGinty, *Interpretation and Dionysos*, 228, note 61.

————. *The Minoan-Mycenaean Religion and its Survival in Greek Religion*. Biblo and Tannen: New York, 1971. For criticism and appreciation of Nilsson, see Guthrie, *Orpheus and Greek Religion*, 144; and Alderink, *Creation and Salvation*, 13. Unfortunately, Nilsson's work has "disturbing racist, sexist, elitist undertones," McGinty, *Dionysos and Interpretation*, 123, 127, 229, notes 74 and 83; Nilsson's work on Dionysos is state of the art, McGinty, *Dionysos and Interpretation*, 104; but Nilsson believed religions are created by defective intelligences using ineffective magical methods of confused associations in dealing with practical problems, McGinty, *Dionysos and Interpretation*, 109;

Nilsson argued that the Greeks viewed the incursion of the cult of Dionysos as an "atavistic reversion" from Anatolia, McGinty, *Dionysos and Interpretation*, 122.

Oxford Classical Dictionary. Oxford: Oxford University Press, 1961. Not quite as good as Smith's, but essential.

Paget, R. F. *In Search of Orpheus*. New York: Roy, 1967. Rogue scholar finds river Styx and possible site of Orphic mysteries. Well translated generous collection of quotes about Orphism and quick introduction to myth and cult by the Indiana Jones of Orphic studies. Alderink writes: "out of touch or interest with the historical and scholarly problems," *Creation and Salvation*, 99.

Parke, H. W. *The Oracles of Zeus: Dodona, Olympia, Ammon*. Cambridge: Harvard University Press, 1967. Parke reminds us that Dodona was a single tree and not a grove. He believes the dove in the tree of Zeus was the ring dove, less common in Greece.

Pausanius. *Description of Greece*. Translated by Anonymous (Thomas Taylor). London, 1824. One of Taylor's clearest translations, with his usual gold mine of notes.

Pepper, Elizabeth and Wilcock, John. *Magical and Mystical Sites: Europe and the British Isles*. Grand Rapids: Phanes Press, 1993. "The largest builidng in Pompeii stood at the southwest end of the forum and was a basilica dedicated to Orpheus. . . . It was at the basilica to Orpheus that the bankers and merchants of Pompeii met to discuss business. Here also judgements were made," 116.

Petrakos, Basil. *Delphi*. Athens: Clio, 1977. An informative guidebook with color photos.

Plassman, J. O. Orpheus: *Altgriechische Mysterien*. Regensburg: 1982. A German translation of the Hymns.

Prumm, Karl. "Die Orphik im Spiegel der neuen Forschung," *Zeitschrift fur katologische Theologie* 78 (1956): 1–40. Survey of research on Orphism recommended by Alderink who summarizes it in *Creation and Salvation*, 7ff, 134.

Raine, Kathleen. *Blake and Tradition*. Princeton: Princeton University Press, 1962. Classic and important two volume study of the influence of Neoplatonism and Orphism on the poetry of the great William Blake. A wealth of beautiful illustrations, analysis and references.

Ronan, Stephen. "Hekate's Inyx." In *Alexandria 1*, edited by David Fideler, 321–335. Grand Rapids: Phanes Press, 1991. Detailed discussion of Hekate's mysterious cult object.

Rooley, Anthony. *Performance: Revealing the Orpheus Within*. Dorset: Element, 1990. Charming and inspiring application of Orphism influenced performance theories and techniques presented by the director of the celebrated Consort of Musicke. A helpful and interesting short discussion of Orphic myth, cult and historical influence from Ficino to Spenser and Dowland.

Smith, Sir William. *Dr. Smith's Classical Dictionary*. London: John Murray, 1894. The holy grail of classical dictionaries is the three volume edition of this one volume abbreviated version. Still better than the Oxford Classical Dictionary despite the lack of modern scholarship.

Taylor, Thomas, trans. *The Hymns of Orpheus*. Los Angeles: Philosophical Research Society, 1981. Venerable but difficult, occasionally beautiful translation with invaluable notes, a long and useful introduction to the life and theology of Orpheus, and numerous quotations from Neoplatonic sources ignored by most scholars. This rhymed version of the Orphic Hymns is the first ever English translation, originally published in 1787.

———. *The Eleusinian and Bacchic Mysteries*. Reprint. San Diego: Wizards Bookshelf, 1980. In this work, first published in 1790, Taylor develops a point he makes in a note to his translation of *Description of Greece* by Pausanius: "... the Orphic hymns which exist at present were the very hymns which were used in the Eleusinian Mysteries." Taylor relies heavily on the Neoplatonists.

Tyrrell, William Blake. *Amazons: A Study in Athenian Mythmaking*. London: John Hopkins, 1984. Comprehensive study of the Amazon myth with focus on Athenian sexual politics and the suppression of matriarchy.

Warden, John, ed. *Orpheus: The Metamorphoses of a Myth.* Toronto: University of Toronto Press, 1982. Collection of essays on the influence of Orphism on the history of western culture. Warden's essay on Ficino is excellent.

West, Martin L. *The Orphic Poems.* Oxford: Oxford University Press, 1983. Study of the Orphic Rhapsodies, a creation myth.

Wilder, Alexander. "Platonic Technology." In *The Platonist* I, II, edited by Thomas Johnson. St. Louis: 1881. An informative short dictionary. *The Platonist* contains other interesting articles and translations by rogue scholars Alexander Wilder and Thomas Johnson. A must for Thomas Taylor fans, with a biography of Taylor and a wealth of reprints and quotes from his work.